THIS IS
N⬤T
A DRILL

THIS IS N🦷T A DRILL

Caring for Your Oral Health with
Category of One Dentistry

DR. SCOTT NAGY, D.D.S

Advantage | Books

Published by Advantage, Charleston, South Carolina.
Member of Advantage Media.

ADVANTAGE is a registered trademark, and the Advantage colophon is a trademark of Advantage Media Group, Inc.

Printed in the United States of America.

10 9 8 7 6 5 4 3 2 1

ISBN: 978-1-64225-745-8 (Paperback)
ISBN: 978-1-64225-744-1 (eBook)

Cover designed by Wesley Strickland.

This publication is designed to provide accurate and authoritative information in regard to the subject matter covered. It is sold with the understanding that the publisher is not engaged in rendering legal, accounting, or other professional services. If legal advice or other expert assistance is required, the services of a competent professional person should be sought.

Advantage Media helps busy entrepreneurs, CEOs, and leaders write and publish a book to grow their business and become the authority in their field. Advantage authors comprise an exclusive community of industry professionals, idea-makers, and thought leaders. Do you have a book idea or manuscript for consideration? We would love to hear from you at **AdvantageMedia.com**.

But First... Gratitude!

Before getting into the core of my book, I want to first recognize and show appreciation for some of the many people that have influenced me, one way or another, directly or indirectly, along the wild & crazy journey to where I stand today.

First and foremost, I have the deepest, most intense gratitude for **Kathy Nagy.** My wife, best friend, biggest fan, awesome mom for our kids, wisest counsel, most authentic advisor and most trusted critic when I need one. She loves me without conditions in spite of knowing my weaknesses and seeing me at my worst. She understands me even when she doesn't understand me (if that makes sense...). Words cannot describe what she means to me and how fortunate and grateful I am to be part of her life. She makes me whole and I am thankful for her energy, her spirit and the life and family that we have created together. I am excited for our future!

Some of the many others that I have deep gratitude and appreciation for:

Gregory and Danielle Nagy: Always my inspiration for working hard and trying to be and do my best.

Thom Davis: A wise "old" detective and model for generosity.

Dr. Bill Carter & Dr. Dennis Kempf: Both models for showing what a kind heart and compassion as a dentist looks like. Thank you for your motivation by example for me to become a dentist.

Shelley Chopak: You get it! Thank you for supporting the vision!

My Future Grandkids and Great-Grandkids: I haven't met you yet but I am working for and fiercely focused on your success in the future. I love you and can't wait to have you as part of our family!

Glenn "Coop" Cooper and Matt Miller: Ferry boat captains that took me under their wings to teach me how to advocate for myself (and goof off when appropriate) when I was Crew (Swab) on the Miller Boat Line   between the Lake Erie Islands.

Jay Geier: Effective coach and Impact Diagram Titan!

Jim Boltz: Genuine and caring. An advisor that counsels with love for people.

Zig Ziglar: If you have experienced Zig, then you know...........

Dr. Duke Heller and Dr. Rob Heller: Amazing mentors in Surgical Implant Dentistry among other life and spiritual lessons. Integrity defined!

Rich Clouse: Financial wizard and trustworthy advisor.

Steve Nagy: Father. Thank you for my work ethic. I did get off my butt and you were right, nobody ever just handed me success!

Last but not least, to the multiple numbers of negative critics that declared that I would never catch my biggest dream of becoming a dentist, thanks for the inspiration and motivation! I did't do it to prove you wrong, I did it to affirm that I was right!

Table of Contents

Part Two:
Your Mouth at Every Age

Part Three:
Sleep Apnea and Snoring

Part One

A Category of One

Introduction

CREATED TO SERVE

*This is not a drill. It's the real deal! Not a
practice run—only the main event.*

—Dr. Scott Nagy

Hello! I'm Dr. Scott Nagy, founder of the Nagy Family Dental Group, a practice I started nearly thirty years ago (at this writing) to fulfill my dream of becoming a dentist near my hometown of Elyria, Ohio. Located just six miles from Lake Erie and 20 miles from Cleveland—it's the place I first envisioned becoming a dentist after graduating from Elyria Catholic High School in 1985. I fiercely pursued that ambition by earning my undergraduate and doctorate degrees at The Ohio State University in Columbus, while working as a dental assistant and hygienist at the Nationwide Children's Hospital Dental Clinic. After that, I practiced dentistry in Columbus for another two years before returning home, determined to establish a special kind of dental practice in the town where I'd grown up. I envisioned offering compassionate and virtually pain-free dentistry to *everyone* seeking dental services in the Cleveland area. Recognizing this was my life's work, I gathered a team of clinically-gifted and like-minded dentists, and we got to work helping dental patients! That was almost three decades ago, and a lot has changed. During that time, my wife Kathy and I watched our two children, Gregory and Danielle grow up as we attended Grace Christian & Missionary Alliance Church in Middleburg Heights. But our dental group's focus on providing the most pain-free dentistry didn't change. And it never will.

Serving by Providing Comfortable Dentistry

We know many people postpone going to the dentist (or avoid it all together) because they've had painful treatment experiences in the past—experiences that have left them with a fear of dentistry. Even tough, active-duty Army Rangers who survived active combat in war zones have told us, "I'd rather be looking down the barrel of a loaded gun than sitting here in this dental chair!" But there's no shame in that. It just shows that fear of dental work is *very* common.

I recently performed dental surgery on a former Marine, for example, who seemed like a really stoic guy. Afterwards, he asked me how long I'd been doing dentistry.

"28 years," I told him. "Why do you ask?"

"Because I literally didn't feel a thing when you numbed me, and I've never had a dentist be able to do that," he replied, looking very surprised and relieved.

Of course, it felt great to hear that. It always does, especially when treating military guys who feel they have to act tough all the time. I treated a lot of these "tough guys" on a mission trip to the Dominican Republic with the Christian Medical and Dental Association (CMDA). One of my first patients was a big enlisted guy in uniform. After my Spanish translator explained he was having some problems with a particular tooth, I examined him and agreed to do the filling he needed. Starting into my normal routine, I gave him an injection to numb his gum, then waited a moment to let it take effect. Suddenly, he touched his cheek, then turned to the translator and began talking to her in very animated Spanish.

"What did he do to me?" He asked her, while glaring at me.

"Oh, he just gave you a shot to make your face numb," the young translator told him.

My patient shook his head and spoke vehemently in Spanish. Apparently, he was insisting I could not have given him a shot because he hadn't felt it, and he couldn't understand why his face was feeling frozen. We talked him through that, and he finally just looked at me with wide eyes and gave me a lop-sided smile.

This is what we mean when we talk about guarding a patient's experience so they don't feel much, if any, discomfort. It's something we can largely control, which is why we put so much intention, effort, and energy into doing that here at Nagy Family Dental Group. Our focus on comfortable dentistry is the reason we're one the few family dental practices in the Northern Ohio area licensed to provide intravenous (I.V.) sedation dentistry. Doing so requires a commitment to continue the rigorous training and licensing we must maintain to offer this kind of pain relief during comprehensive dental work, such as implants. But whatever the procedure, we really enjoy helping people with pain-free sedation because it works so well. In fact, we frequently provide sedation for patients referred by other doctors—some over an hour away—so patients can relax during their dental treatments.

Serving to Grow or Growing to Serve?

The reason we prioritize dental pain relief can be summed up in the word *service*. To be honest, serving patients in this way is our top priority and our biggest motivator. In other words, we want to be successful and expand to increase the number of people we can serve, not because we want to get paid more. This caring, patient-first approach is what sets us apart as we provide the virtually painless techniques and technology available for the wide array of dental services we offer:

- General Dentistry

- Cosmetic Dentistry

- Restorative Dentistry

- Children's Dentistry

- Sleep Apnea Treatment

- Dental Implants

- Sedation Dentistry

- BOTOX®

- Facial Esthetics

- Six Month Smiles®

- Invisalign®

This *putting-others-first* priority is also reflected in the way our dental group delivers the enhanced patient comfort and safety benefits of using the newest dental technologies, including a state-of-the art cone beam volumetric tomography x-ray (CBCT) unit, digital oral scanner, and laser equipment that facilitates quick, pain-free treatment and rapid healing. We're also proud to offer patients our dental implant expertise from the Midwest Implant Institute.

But no matter what kind of dentistry is needed, helping *everyone* access excellent dental treatment in the most optimal, comfortable way possible is our number one purpose and goal. The more people we see and connect with at our practice, the more people we can serve. This simple and beautiful equation expresses our core value: the belief that *we're all built to serve*, and that we've been made that way by our Creator with the express purpose of creating a connection to other people. In fact, when you think about it, there's no job or work role that doesn't serve somebody else, including dentistry. And we've built our practice on this premise of serving and caring for others.

Serving from the Heart

Our commitment to caring and serving includes supporting the operation of our free dental clinic, Salt and Light, which we started in our community for those who can't afford to pay for dental treatment. It's housed in our original practice building and every clinician we hire must contractually agree to donate some of their work hours (volunteer time) to that clinic or we don't hire them. This prerequisite has actually turned out to be a great litmus test. If a doctor or technician doesn't want to serve the community in this way, we know they're not going to be a good fit for a practice where we've prioritized the kind of compassionate dentistry that seeks to meet the needs of others *first*.

What does that mean for you as a patient? It means you'll meet *kinder, more caring* dentists at our practice who will treat you like an honored guest as soon as you walk through our doors. It also means we'll work very hard to guard your experience while you're with us at the clinic. From your very first appointment, you become a member of our practice family that we genuinely care about, so we'll never hurry you into a closed-off cubicle where there's barely room for a dental chair with a tiny sink and an overhead "searchlight" that's too bright. Instead, we'll welcome you into treatment spaces having an open-design that's spacious and relaxing so you won't feel claustrophobic and vulnerable during treatment. This kind of caring attention-to-detail is the basis of our culture and our seven core values. In other words, we're *caring people,* caring for others. We must be getting that right, because our patients often tell us how comfortable they feel after treatment.

Our Seven Core Values

1. Service
2. Loyalty
3. Integrity
4. Teamwork
5. Generosity
6. Stewardship
7. Proactive Gratitude

Many will say, "I've never had a dental appointment that was so comfortable and relaxing!"

Hearing that is very rewarding because the words "comfortable, relaxing" and "dentist" aren't usually linked!

Serving that's Relational Instead of Transactional

Our practice environment is so relaxing because our team prioritizes being *relational* versus transactional. Instead of putting a process first, being relational means putting your individual needs as a patient first. If you come in with a broken tooth, for example, we won't hustle you into the chair, fix your tooth, and then hurry you out the door with a "See you later!" Being relational means taking the time to really listen and assess your individual feelings and needs, then confirming with you that we understand your preferences. We not only want to know what makes you comfortable but *uncomfortable* too—so we can avoid doing it! This is the basis of our relational approach as healers and healthcare providers, and the rewards are more satisfying than the transactional approach of fixing teeth to get wealthy. We want to build relationships and get to know people as we treat them, rather than providing an impersonal service. Sometimes that makes sticking to a treatment schedule more challenging, but it's worth it! In fact, the continuing push for automation may mean robots will be doing our job at some point, but we don't think their patients will feel cared for the way ours do before, during, and after their treatment.

If a dental practice has a transactional environment, it may feel more like a well-oiled machine than a place of healing and restoration. It might seem impersonal (and even scary) when you hear the dreaded words: *This will only hurt for a second. Here we go!* This kind of approach makes it clear who has all the control and who is vulnerable and powerless—the hapless patient! These poor patients feel they have no choice in the matter, and they have to do whatever the doctor orders. *The doctor says it's gonna hurt—so it's gonna hurt*, they think. They surrender control to the person that's providing the treatment. And if there's no relational dimension between the doctor and their patient in that moment of vulnerability, it's going to intensify that patient's anxiety, powerlessness, and discomfort when they experience any kind of pain during treatment. That's just human nature. And this common scenario is what creates most of the dental apprehension afflicting so many people. Knowing that is why we prioritize our relationship with you as a patient above all else. That means we'll empower you and put you in control of how you receive treatment by letting you choose the pace.

Although these advantages set our practice apart from many others, our focus on *serving* is what makes it most unique. This aspect of healing transcends our clinical expertise and advanced equipment. A spirit of compassionate service permeates every patient interaction, and our patients can sense it. We've made this our priority because we know the majority of our patients are probably going to be feeling a bit nervous when they see us for dental work. That's normal, of course. Coming in for dental treatment *usually* makes people feel vulnerable and anxious about pain. And this is the reason we work so hard to eliminate dental discomfort. Our compassion is tangible and reassuring to patients who often walk through our clinic's doors feeling fearful about their impending dental work or exam. An awareness of that reality is what motivates us to provide treatment that's comforting and relational for every one of our patients. And we take whatever appointment time is necessary to accomplish that.

Another aspect of our practice's culture of serving is the joy we feel using our time and talent to benefit those who need our expertise. Each member of our team has been experientially trained to understand that for themselves because we believe we're *all* meant to serve others to the absolute best of our abilities using our time, resources, and talent. Doing so is the reason we consider ourselves *healers* rather than medical technicians who are simply focused on fixing your teeth the way an auto mechanic would fix your car.

Serving with a Holistic Approach

Since the whole body is interconnected, healing issues with your mouth and jaw have far-reaching implications. This is especially true if your breathing stops intermittently during sleep due to an obstructed airway. Called obstructive sleep apnea (OSA), it usually occurs because soft tissue in the back of the throat collapses and temporarily blocks the airway (and breathing) during sleep. Depending on how many episodes of OSA occur in an hour, the condition is considered mild (5–15), moderate (15–30), or severe (30 or more). These episodes can occur hundreds of times each night and really hurt your health by robbing your body of the oxygen it needs to thrive. Although OSA isn't the only form of sleep apnea, it causes over 80% of all cases.

Disordered breathing can involve the nasal airway too. When people can't breathe through their noses, it's called upper airway resistance syndrome. This is the main cause of mouth breathing, something that's detrimental to maintaining a healthy jaw position. And inhaling air through your mouth and directly into your lungs instead of through your nose (where it's filtered, hydrated, and heated) has been linked to a higher incidence of asthma. Mouth breathing is also associated with the cheek pain triggered by jaw clenching and tooth grinding. Patients often come to see me thinking there's something wrong with their temporomandibular joints (TMJ) when it's really their breathing problems that are to blame.

Serving with our Dental Sleep Medicine Center

Sleep apnea afflicts all age groups and is so widespread, I've become a certified Diplomat for the American Sleep and Breathing Academy. And since it worsens over time, we're on a crusade to spread awareness about the dangers of sleep apnea so more dentists will assess their patients for the condition like we do. It's vital that dentists and patients understand how sleep apnea can harm every aspect of a person's health and longevity in very serious ways. Apnea has even been linked to cardiovascular symptoms such as high blood pressure, stroke, heart failure, irregular heartbeats, and heart attacks. Unfortunately, I learned that the hard way from my own battle with undiagnosed sleep apnea.

Several years ago, I began feeling a lot of fatigue and went to see a general internist. Tests showed my red blood cells were so abnormally large they couldn't flow properly through my blood vessels. *No wonder I'm so tired all the time*, I thought. I was told the enlargement of my red blood cells meant I had one of two disorders: either cancer or another condition associated with poor oxygenation of the blood. Fortunately, it turned out to be the latter due to my undiagnosed OSA, and discovering it probably saved my life! My brain (and everything else) had been starved of oxygen for so long it had orchestrated the biochemical changes that had made my red blood cells larger as a coping mechanism. Like so many, I hadn't realized my daytime drowsiness, slightly-recessed jaw, nasal stuffiness, and snoring were all small signs pointing to a really big problem. Following the adage, "Physician, heal thyself," I've been following the same treatment protocol we use with our patients to resolve my own OSA. Getting treated for sleep apnea has been a game changer for me, as it has been for so many of our patients whose breathing has been normalized.

The bottom line is that untreated apnea can shorten a person's life, and people need to take the condition seriously. The person who drove to our sleep center from Columbus, Ohio *two hours away* certainly did. He was eager to get relief from the disrupted breathing that was robbing him of the sleep he so desperately needed to live a normal life. After listening carefully to that patient's concerns, I examined the size and shape of his jaw arches. I know a narrow upper jaw and/or recessed lower jaw can abnormally confine the tongue in a way that causes OSA or nasal airway problems. The roof of his mouth proved to be more vaulted than normal as I expected. I also saw the tell-tale "scallop" patterns on either side of his tongue (impressions left by the teeth) that indicated his tongue didn't have the room it needed due to his jaw configuration. After holding up a hand-held mirror to show him, I explained it was like keeping a six-foot tiger in a three-foot cage, with the jaws being the cage and the tongue being the tiger. I also reassured him we could treat the problem successfully. He was relieved to hear I could help him breathe and sleep normally again. And he was even happier when he heard his treatment wouldn't require surgery, but a variety of comfortable, non-surgical treatments that would only take about 16–18 months. I told him he would definitely know his treatment was working when he started waking up in the morning thinking, *Man, I feel great!*

Are you wondering whether sleep apnea could be affecting you too? You can actually look in the mirror and check for those impressions on your tongue right now. If you see the scallop pattern I just described, please see a dental sleep apnea specialist as soon as possible. They will want to check whether you've been experiencing any of the other common symptoms of OSA:

- Waking up with a sore/dry throat

- Habitual snoring

- Being awakened by a choking or gasping sensation

- Drowsiness or fatigue during the day

- Morning headaches

- Restless sleep

- Poor memory, mood changes, low libido

- Recurrent waking or insomnia

Having these symptoms means a sleep test is definitely needed, and you can do that at a dental sleep center like mine. If testing indicates you have sleep apnea, it would be wise to start your treatment as soon as possible. That's so critically important because OSA can cause such a serious array of health problems including diabetes, depression, and worsening of attention-deficit with hyper-activity disorder (ADHD).

In the past, dentists have typically tried to manage the separate symptoms of sleep apnea I listed without realizing their patients had apnea and required treatment. Some dentists recommend their patients wear "snore guard" appliances to curb snoring, for example, but this doesn't address the root cause of their snoring. Using the appliance to bring the lower jaw forward does manage the problem by opening the airway, but it doesn't treat the root cause of snoring. This requires changing the size, shape, and volume of the airway which is what we're doing at our practice. As a person with apnea falls asleep, they'll progress through several abnormal breathing stages: mouth breathing is first, noisy breathing is second, then snoring happens last—completing the disordered breathing cycle that disrupts sleep.

Serving to give you a Better Quality of Life

Fortunately, a growing number of dentists now know it's important to assess patients for underlying apnea, instead of treating its many symptoms separately. They also know, as we do, that reparative, REM sleep is essential to flush toxins from the brain and heal the body and mind. Restorative sleep is also when the key hormone serotonin is released to initiate feelings of wellbeing. This happiness hormone not only helps normalize sleeping and digestion but promotes communication between brain cells and the nervous system. I hope knowing you can have a healthy, beautiful smile and feel good too will motivate you to see a dentist who will assess you for sleep apnea. This is what really sets a practice like ours apart. If you come to see us for a preventive check or cleaning or because you or your child's tooth is in need of a filling or repair, we'll certainly take care of that. But we'll also look at you or your child's jaws and airways to check for signs of the disrupted breathing that causes sleep apnea.

Serving Collaboratively with other Doctors

Up until a few years ago, we never screened our patients for any type of breathing disorder. No dentists did, because we simply didn't know it was an issue. We were always looking inside our patients' mouths and seeing their airways without realizing the key to many systemic health problems was right in front of us. Now, looking back, I wonder how many older patients might still be alive if we dentists had known to check them for OSA. With that in mind, I'm very grateful a growing awareness of sleep apnea and other breathing problems has caused such a huge paradigm shift among dentists all over the world. We no longer focus solely on the health of the oral cavity, but on how it's connected to the health of the whole body.

As a result, practices like ours are now collaborating with a medical network of physicians with different specialties, and we're all learning from one another. Because so many serious cases are going undiagnosed, some sleep physicians have characterized sleep-disordered breathing and obstructive sleep apnea as a public health crisis.

Sleep apnea affects all age groups, even the very young, but its negative impact on body oxygenation and restorative sleep can become increasingly destructive to health when it's not treated. Some of our patients are young children who have the symptoms of sleep apnea and the abnormal jaw that often accompanies it. They can't give up their thumb-sucking habit (it's an instinctual form of self-treatment), tooth grinding, or open mouth position. Among older patients, sleep apnea can cause increased memory loss and a host of other chronic ailments that tend to grow worse over time.

Once they've learned about the symptoms of sleep apnea and have been treated, some of these older patients confide they think their spouses (who had died previously from heart attacks or stroke) probably had apnea too. It's sobering for them to think their loved ones might have lived many years longer with the proper sleep apnea diagnosis and treatment. To provide that now, our practice has created a separate sleep apnea space. This kind of practice isn't commonly available yet, but we sincerely hope other dentists will commit to acquiring the expertise necessary to detect and treat apnea in their patients. That way, the apnea patient I saw won't have to make the two-hour drive from Columbus! So what are *you* waiting for? We're here to serve you with comfortable, caring, and comprehensive dentistry that will enhance your overall health, while giving you the kind of healthy smile that never goes out of style.

Chapter One

THE PATIENT-CENTRIC PHILOSOPHY

Five Reasons People Don't Like Doctor Visits

From the Huffington Post

1. The doctor doesn't listen

2. The long wait

3. The doctor doesn't care

4. The doctor makes too much money

5. My dog gets more respect

The system we have created in our office is what's called the Patient-Centric Model. The entire experience is crafted around putting the patient first, with predetermined steps that include speed when speed is necessary, clear communication, and treatment that is well above the norm.

Words that Describe a Patient-Centric Model

Comfortable

Relaxed

Understood

Important

Satisfied

Listened to

Cared for

Respected

Creating a Five-Star Experience

When you walk into our office, our focus is on getting you to where you need to be as fast as possible, streamlining paperwork so that there's time for true comfort and relaxation. To accomplish this, we extensively train our team on what both the patient and the doctor require so there are as few hiccups in the process as possible.

This attention to detail and process goes well beyond the evident. For instance:

- ***Answering the Phone Right Away***. This may seem obvious, but try calling your physician right now. If you're like most, your call was probably received by an automated answering service that made you pick a number, and then another number, and possibly even a third number, just so you can leave a message on an answering machine. This is not the case at our office. Our phones are answered quickly by a real person so that we can address your needs promptly.

- **Flexible Schedule**. We strive to keep flexibility in our schedule so that if the need occurs, we can see you quickly—if not the same day—at a time that's as convenient as possible.

- **Clean Spaces**. Every space associated with our office, from our parking area to the storage closet, is kept clean and in good condition. The sign for our office is easy to read from the street, so you know you're at the right place, and parking for new patients is reserved up front. The common areas and restrooms are clean and comfortable, and lightly scented so that they don't smell medical while at the same time, not overpoweringly fragrant. And there's no such thing as a worn or dirty surface in our office space. We make it a point to keep *all* glass surfaces clean, the paint fresh, and the furniture in good, clean condition.

- **Reception Desk**. Gone are the days of the non-responsive front desk person behind a tiny sliding glass window. Not only have we removed the window, but the front desk is also open and uncluttered, with a smiling front desk operator that greets you the moment you walk up. There is no waiting for someone to get off the phone and, if you were able to fill out our online forms ahead of time (sent directly to your preferred email address), there's usually no clipboard, either.

- ***Waiting Room***. The waiting room is not only clean and tidy, but it's also completely devoid of old, worn, and rumpled magazines. Instead, there's a wide variety of reading material for all ages, along with a comfortably placed television (on low volume with captions, on a non-news channel that *isn't* discussing medical or dental procedures), free wi-fi, and a toy box for children with toys that are cleaned daily. We also offer chilled bottled water on request, along with other patient amenities.

- ***Treatment Rooms***. We understand that the fear factor for dental offices is real and pervasive in our society. For that reason, when you walk into a treatment room, you're not going to see a lot of medical equipment sitting out. Instead, we use soft lighting, tasteful decorations, and comfortable furniture to create a more relaxed experience.

- ***Our Appearance***. This may not seem like an obvious importance, but we have several rules regarding the appearance of staff and doctors in our office. Uniforms must fit correctly—neither too tight nor too loose—and dentists must wear dress clothes with a clean, white lab coat. Everyone, from the front desk to the doctor, must be well-groomed with tattoos covered and any body piercings removed. It may not seem like a lot, but a clean and tidy appearance—from the rooms to the staff and even the doctor—lets our clients know that we pay attention to detail, and that every detail gets professional treatment.

Perception Is Everything

A story I've often heard attributed to Don Burr, founder of the former People Express Airlines, does an excellent job of pointing out the importance of attention to every detail.

Picture yourself the last time you had to fly somewhere. Imagine you had a pretty ideal experience this time around—you checked in early online, the line for security was minimal, and your gate was conveniently close to a cafe with clean, available tables. When they called your flight, you got onboard without a hitch, found a spot for your luggage right over your seat, and got into your seat without stepping over two other people or ticking off the other passengers around you.

Everything was going brilliantly until you sat down and unfolded the tray table and there, on the surface of the table, was a huge, crusty food stain. In that moment, you suddenly became convinced that the pilot was incompetent, the wings were held on with duct tape and the engine was one decrepit shiver from bursting into flame.

Perception is everything, and if we aren't paying attention to detail, then dentists can be rest assured that their clients *are*.

Everything about your visit, from the moment you arrive, should feel like a five-star experience.

A fair number of patient satisfaction surveys suggest that while patients may like their doctor, they are most dissatisfied with the treatment they received from supporting team members. This is why our focus is a complete 180 degrees from the typical medical office experience—we spend an enormous amount of energy and effort making sure that our team is always present and aware of our clients' needs. Our staff know—and agree—that their needs come second to the needs of our patients.

From the moment you walk in the door, your experience dictates your relationship with us. Creating the best first impression requires substantial energy and effort, but if the end result is that our clients feel more comfortable, less fearful, and more respected by our doctors and staff, then it's all worth it.

Category of One

What is a "category of one" dental practice?

It's a dental practice that values the power of distinction versus the cost of blending in. It's one that goes above and beyond for its patients, creating an environment that's difficult—if not impossible—for others to duplicate.

This distinction doesn't just apply to our physical building, however. It's also found in how we treat our patients and in the services we provide. For our patients, we want to give them the kind of smile that doesn't just serve its purpose, but stands out. A "category of one" company is, at all times, a reflection of the utmost quality in all aspects of its operation and it's this type of practice that we aim to exemplify every day.

Chapter Two

WHAT IS AN UNHEALTHY SMILE COSTING YOU?

As humans go, our greatest fears are pretty specific: there's extinction, of course, as well as physical injury, loss of autonomy, separation, and ego-death.[1] If you were to put these in order, extinction would be the most powerful, followed by the others in this same order, ending in ego-death, which can also be described as "embarrassment, humiliation, or any other form of strong self-disapproval."

So, where does "fear of dentistry" fall in this? It depends on how you view a dentist visit. More than likely, it falls first under the fear of physical injury—that we'll somehow feel pain during our visit. This isn't an uncommon fear. In fact, about 75 percent of all U.S. citizens have

---

1   Karl Albrecht, "The (Only) 5 Fears We All Share," Psychology today, last modified March 22, 2012, https://www.psychologytoday.com/blog/brainsnacks/201203/the-only-5-fears-we-all-share

some degree of fear of the dentist, from mild to severe, with anywhere between 5 and 10 percent of the population experiencing true dental phobia, meaning that they'll avoid a dentist's office at all costs.[2]

What is that "cost," by the way? What is fear costing us when we won't go to the dentist because our gums bleed a little when we brush or because that one tooth is really starting to ache more often?

What are the opportunity costs of fear?

When we look back at things we've done in life that we were initially afraid of, we most often find that those fears were simply built up in our own head.

Take Geoff's story, for instance. At forty-one years old, he was only able to visit a dentist under IV sedation, and had been that way for at least twenty-five years. For Geoff, this severely limited the dentists he could go to, and meant that he only saw them when something was wrong. In this particular case, he arrived at a dental hospital with tooth pain and an examination showed that he had no less than three teeth that needed to come out. After he had them extracted under sedation, however, Geoff was able to undergo therapy that allowed him to slowly ease into a dental office and eventually have a tooth restored and two cavities filled with just a local anesthetic; with no IV and fully conscious.[3]

If Geoff had been able to deal with his fear earlier in life and simply visited his dentist regularly, it's likely he never would have needed such extensive work done. That is, in a nutshell, a whole bunch of opportunity costs—by choosing to let fear keep him from the dentist, it cost

---

2 Peter Milgrom, Philip Weinstein, and Tracy Getz, *Treating Fearful Dental Patients: A Patient Management Handbook, 2nd Edition* (Seattle, WA: University of Washington, Cont, 1995)

3 K.I. Wilson and J.G. Davies, "A joint approach to treating dental phobics between community dental services and specialist psychotherapy services – a single case report," *British Dental Journal* 190, no. 8 (April 2001): 431–2, https://doi.org/10.1038/sj.bdj.4800993a

24 · DR. SCOTT NAGY, D.D.S.

him twenty-five years of proactive dental visits, tooth pain from lack of treatment, dental damage, and likely the impact to his self-esteem for a quarter of a century because of a poor smile.

When you think back on your own life, it's likely there are more than a few instances where you had to walk through your fear instead of backing away from it—and you probably found out that you'd made it a lot more frightening in your own head than it was in actuality.

Are Bad Teeth Telling Your Life Story?

Your smile tells your life story faster than any other means known to humanity. First impressions are made in milliseconds, and while research is still trying to pinpoint all the details of how we're able to assess people so quickly, we do know that common facial features play an incredible role in other people's initial—and lasting—perception of you.

"A first glance at a person's face often leaves a lasting impression," writes psychologist Vivian Diller in a July 2012 article for *Psychology Today*. "Facial features are more often remembered following initial interactions than people's bodies or even their personality traits."

Diller goes on to note several conclusions that people make based on their first impression of our eyes, nose, skin, and hair, as well as our smile and our teeth, all of which are viewed and assessed in less than a second.

"A person's smile is the feature that elicits the most immediate and positive reaction from others," Diller states. "People who have a spontaneous and natural smile … send an inviting message to others. It says 'come join me, talk to me.' An unsmiling face, however, can say, 'I'm not interested.' A frown says, 'go away.'"

Teeth, too, leave a strong impression. "While we may not all have dazzling straight pearly whites, having good oral hygiene goes along with the positive impact that a great smile brings," writes Diller. "Severely crooked or yellowing teeth can imply you are a smoker or heavy drinker. Mottled teeth can reflect certain illnesses, poor nutrition, or an eating disorder. Fresh and bright teeth generally suggest that you are someone with a healthy lifestyle and good grooming habits."

Photogenic or Not, Good Teeth Matter

Good teeth are a hot topic on the acting website Backstage.com. In an article titled "Nothing But the Tooth," actors speak to how improvements to their smiles made significant differences in their careers.

"Before I got my teeth whitened, they [casting directors] made comments suggesting that I was not going to be on TV," said actress Sonora Chase. "That has changed."

Actress Jessica Delfino also shared that a quality veneer made all the difference in her performing career, taking her from being self-conscious about a poorly repaired front tooth to having the confidence to take on the "perfection-loving media."

According to Dr. Michelle Callahan, "Whether we like it or not, we are often judged by our appearance...your smile has more of an effect on what others perceive about you than you think."

In a perception study conducted by marketing research firm Kelton, more than a thousand participants were asked to give their honest opinion on the people in a variety of images, and what they found was that those with straight teeth appeared to have more desirable qualities than those with crooked teeth, including the snap judgment that they were "happy" and "professionally successful."

In comparison to people with crooked teeth, the perception study also noted that Americans perceive those with straight teeth as being:

- 45 percent more likely to get a job
- 58 percent more successful
- 57 percent more likely to get a date
- 47 percent more likely to be viewed as healthy

Additionally, close to three in five Americans would rather have a nice smile than clear skin, and 87 percent would give up something for a year if it meant having a nice smile for the rest of their life.

So what story is your smile telling others? And just as importantly, how is that story affecting your *life story* going forward?

"Research clearly shows that having decayed or missing teeth has a strong negative impact on self-esteem," notes psychologist Daniel W. McNeil, PhD. "It also has an impact on employability."[4]

Bad Teeth, No Job

When the American Dental Association took a look at oral health and well-being in the United States in 2015, it uncovered some

---

4   Rebecca A. Clay, "Drilling down on dental fears," *Monitor on Psychology* 47, no. 3 (March 2016): 60, http://www.apa.org/monitor/2016/03/dental-fears.aspx

alarming statistics. Young adults were almost neck-and-neck with low income adults in agreeing that "the appearance of my mouth and teeth affects my ability to interview for a job," and one in four adults avoid smiling due to the condition of their mouth and teeth. Judging by what we just learned from psychologist Vivian Diller, this means that a quarter of adults are unintentionally hurting the first impression they give others just because they're too embarrassed to smile.

For a case in point, just look at the story of "Shelly" as reported by the Deseret News in Salt Lake City, Utah.

In 2012, a counseling office in Salt Lake City was looking for a front desk employee and while they were getting plenty of applicants, none met all of their specific qualifications. Then, Shelly arrived at the office as a temp. A thirty-five-year-old mother of three, she was reportedly "pleasant to work with, competent, and kind to the patients." In fact, another front desk employee urged leadership to hire Shelly on permanently. Yet, when her temp position ended, the company chose not to bring her on.

When asked why Shelly wasn't hired, employees were apparently told that it was because she had bucked, crooked teeth.

"He [the office manager] said it wasn't the image we wanted to project at our clinic," said one of the front desk employees.[5]

Image Is the New Communication

Communication is becoming more and more image-focused, with social media reflecting this through a massive uptick in video messaging. As of 2017, more than 70 percent of Gen-Z (those born after 1995) spent

5   Mercedes White, "No teeth means no job," Deseret News, last modified December 27, 2012, https://www.deseretnews.com/article/865569512/No-teeth-means-no-job-How-poor-oral-health-impacts-job-prospects.html

more than three hours a day watching videos online, and their social platforms of choice, such as SnapChat and Whisper, are almost solely image and video-based.[6]

While most employers aren't as obvious about their motivations in hiring or not hiring certain individuals, you can be certain that a good smile is going to play a big part in other people's first and ongoing impression of you: a factor that a woman in California was well aware of as she sat outside of a state dental clinic overnight.

At fifty-three years old, Patty knew she needed dental work if she was going to land a job. As she waited outside of the clinic, she told an NBC news reporter about her five broken teeth, three cavities and gum abscess, and how the pain was only part of the reason she was there—she knew the condition of her teeth was an important part of the hiring process.

"I really don't smile a lot," she told the reporter. "I know that when you have a job, you want to have a pleasant attitude and you've got to smile and be friendly."

The report went on to quote Dr. Susan Hyde, a dentist and population scientist at the University of California in San Francisco, "If you want to portray someone as being wicked, they have missing front teeth. If they're ignorant, they have buck teeth. Even from a very early age, we associate how one presents their oral health with all kinds of biases that reflect some of the social biases that we have."

Dr. Lindsey Robinson, dentist and president of the California Dental Association, added, "Customer service jobs, good entry-level

6   Nelson Granados, "Gen Z Media Consumption: It's A Lifestyle, Not Just Entertainment," Media & Entertainment, Forbes, last modified June 20, 2017, https://www.forbes.com/sites/nelsongranados/2017/06/20/gen-z-media-consumption-its-a-lifestyle-not-just-entertainment/

jobs ... they're not available to people who have lost the basic ability to smile, to function, to chew properly."[7]

But the chain of consequences resulting from bad teeth doesn't stop here. Poor dental health can also affect your immediate health, and apart from making it difficult to work when you're not feeling well, it can affect your long-term wellbeing and can even result in death.

A Heart Attack ... and Diabetes, Stroke, and Cardiovascular Disease ... Waiting to Happen

In 2007, a twelve-year-old boy in Washington, D.C. died from a toothache. It was a combination of unfortunate circumstances that led to the tragic event, but ultimately, what could have been an $80 routine extraction ended up costing him his life. His family paid close to $250,000 in medical care, including brain surgery in an attempt to save the boy from the infection that had spread from a tooth abscess into his brain.[8]

This is an extreme instance, but the fact is that bacteria, which accumulate quickly in the mouth as they feed on the food particles surrounding un-brushed teeth, have instant access to the blood-stream through the inflamed gums that occur with periodontal disease. These bacteria don't go through any filtering process, either, as they would if they entered the body through the lungs, stomach, ears or nose. In other words, inflammation, the gaps created by a

---

7   Jonel Aleccia, "Bad teeth, broken dreams: Lack of dental care keeps many out of jobs," NBC News, last modified June 12, 2013, https://www.nbcnews.com/feature/in-plain-sight/bad-teeth-broken-dreams-lack-dental-care-keeps-many-out-v18906511

8   Mary Otto, "For Want of a Dentist," Washington Post, last modified February 28, 2007, http://www.washingtonpost.com/wp-dyn/content/article/2007/02/27/AR2007022702116.html

receding gum line, and other untreated dental conditions, are akin to having an un-bandaged open wound on your body. Those bacteria can jump right in and start wreaking havoc, which is why researchers are discovering that there are more diseases than just the obvious ones associated with poor dental health.

The following links between poor dental health and disease are described in depth by the National Institute of Health's report "Oral Health in America: A Report of the Surgeon General": https://www. nidcr.nih.gov/DataStatistics/SurgeonGeneral/sgr/home.htm

- **COPD**. COPD, or chronic obstructive pulmonary disease, is caused by chronic bronchitis, emphysema, or recurring respiratory infection, and has been associated with periodontal disease due to bacterial pneumonia living in the mouth and making its way into the airway.

- **Diabetes**. Periodontitis has been linked to diabetes—both types 1 and 2—so often that it's now being referred to as one of the main complications of diabetes. Reports have suggested that it's a two-way street for these diseases, as well—that diabetics are more likely to get periodontal disease, and periodontal disease may have a negative impact on glycemic control.

- **Heart Disease and Stroke**. Evidence is continuing to grow on the relationship between infectious agents and systemic diseases, with certain bacteria that thrive in dental infections being identified as potentially linked to heart disease. For example, as we said earlier, bacteria or viruses in the mouth can get directly into the blood stream, where they can cause inflammation, blood clots, and narrowing of the arteries.

- ***Preterm Birth and Low Birth Weight***. Bacterial infection in the mouth may contribute to adverse pregnancy outcomes, as the harmful bacteria and other toxins created by the infection can get into the blood, cross the placenta, and harm the fetus. Additionally, the reaction of the mother's immune system to the infection could directly or indirectly interfere with growth and/or delivery.

This Isn't Just About Teeth—It's About the Rest of Your Life

This book isn't about promoting dentistry. It's about helping you discover the long-term opportunity costs of fear and the importance of being proactive about the health of your smile.

The first step is understanding the importance of a healthy mouth, which you should have a better idea of after reading this book. The next step? Understanding that when you're not healthy, you're not living at your full potential.

C h a p t e r   T h r e e

UNLEASHING HUMAN POTENTIAL

At the age of fourteen, Susan still remembers the conversation that took place between her dentist and her parents, when her dentist first urged them to take her to an orthodontist. There was some medical terminology batted about, but one line stuck with her so clearly that she can still hear her dentist saying it today; "If you don't do something now, we'll probably have to break her jaw when she's older."

If she hadn't heard her dentist say that, she might have fussed a little more about the braces her orthodontist fitted her with, but instead she took it all in stride and even switched out her bracket bands to reflect the holidays as they went by. A little over a year later, the braces came off and everyone in the office "ooh"ed and "ahh"ed over her beautiful smile.

Fast forward to a little over two decades later and thirty-seven-year-old Susan couldn't quite remember when she stopped wearing her retainer, though she was sure it was within a year or two after getting her braces off, and certainly before she went to college. Consequently, her teeth had drifted to the point where she could noticeably tell a difference in how they sat in her mouth.

One of the issues people face when it comes to maintaining a healthy smile is the lack of clarity around the natural aging process and its impact on your teeth. Orthodontic relapse is a condition that a lot of post-braces patients fall victim to, and one that we see in the dental office pretty frequently. The issue is that people rarely understand the importance of wearing a retainer and the fact that time and other dental conditions down the road can all affect the hard work that your doctors put into that straight smile so many years ago.

After braces, teeth need at least one year to stabilize and get used to their new positions in the jaw. This is when retainer wear is at its most important—to protect the teeth from relapsing into their former positions and allow them time to solidify in their new positions in the jaws. If a retainer isn't worn, or is worn infrequently, during this time, the teeth may shift and if the patient doesn't visit her dentist, she may not notice that shift for some time.

Even if a retainer is worn for at least a year, after the patient stops wearing it, the teeth once again fall victim to outside—and inside—influences. Teeth grinding, for instance, can place strain on the teeth of the upper jaw, and tooth loss can cause the remaining teeth to drift into the vacant spot. Internal influences could be genetics, which can prompt your teeth to shift, for instance, or gum disease can cause the structure to weaken.

And then there's simply the age factor. As we age, pressures on the teeth can cause them to shift, so even if Susan did wear her retainer for a few years after braces, twenty years is a long time for teeth to react to any influences, internal or external.

In neglecting her teeth, Susan neglected the potential that straight teeth could have resulted in. Apart from generally giving her a healthier appearance, straight teeth also create a healthier mouth in actuality—with straight teeth, there are fewer places for food and bacteria to hide, making it easier to brush. And straight teeth also make chewing easier, which means less strain on the jaw, which means avoiding jaw joint issues down the road.

It's like the old adage "for want of a nail, the kingdom was lost." By not maintaining a healthy smile and being proactive about it, we open the gates to numerous problems down the road. For Susan, drifting teeth meant that they were sitting in less-than-ideal positions in her mouth, making them harder to brush, which meant more bacterial buildup. And more bacterial buildup can cause inflammation of the gums. Inflammation leads to gingivitis, gingivitis leads to periodontal disease and periodontal disease leads to … well, you read the last chapter, right? It could potentially lead to anything from heart disease to death.

All for the want of proactive, preventive dental care.

Hitting the Reset Button On Your Smile

Unlike many things in life, you have the option of hitting the reset button on your smile. It doesn't matter if you've smoked your whole life or if illegal drug use has caused most of your teeth to rot out—whatever you've done, technology and advancements in dental science have made it possible to rebuild just about any smile.

We live in a world today where photos are uploaded by the billions every single day. In 2014, for instance, it was estimated that every two minutes, the same number of photos were uploaded to the Internet as existed in the world one hundred and fifty years ago. This is a world where you can no longer hide your smile.[9] The camera is on you constantly and whether or not you realize it, it's having an impact on the course of your life. People make snap judgments based on the images they see of you, and based on their first 0.1 seconds of interacting with you. You're regularly being assessed in situations and under circumstances where you cannot speak for yourself—your image is doing all of the talking.

I'm aware this probably sounds superficial, but regardless of our better efforts, we're still a superficial species. Our instincts still react the same way they did eons ago—an attractive smile still triggers the selection of a mate. It still inclines us to like or trust someone more. Genuine smiles, also called Duchenne smiles—the ones that get you to use those little muscles around your eyes—also signal to others that you're focusing on just them, which in turn encourages them to cooperate with you.[10]

At the same time, the way you feel about your smile also influences your own perception of self. Your self-concept is determined, many times, by the way you look at yourself in the mirror. Do you smile at yourself from ear to ear or do you frown in an effort to conceal your imperfect grin? That perception lives with you and reflects outward, whether you realize it or not, affecting not only your own happiness, but the happiness you could be generating in others.

---

9   Rose Eveleth, "How Many Photographs of You Are Out There In The World?" The Atlantic, last modified November 2, 2015, https://www.theatlantic.com/technology/archive/2015/11/how-many-photographs-of-you-are-out-there-in-the-world/413389/

10   Gil Greengross, "Want to Increase Trust in Others? Just Smile," Psychology Today, last modified April 30, 2015, https://www.psychologytoday.com/blog/humor-sapiens/201504/want-increase-trust-in-others-just-smile-0

There is no doubt that a bright and vibrant smile can do more to drive happiness in someone's life than you would think on the surface. When you think about it, what are the things you could do in life that will ultimately drive happiness? Most likely, the majority of those things can be traced back to your ability to smile.

What Makes Us Happy?

Research shows that around 40 percent of our own happiness is under our control. So what can you do to make yourself happier - and how do those behaviors relate to your smile?

1. Strong relationships with people you trust
2. Good income / paying bills without stress
3. Taking the time to think about the good things in life
4. Performing voluntary acts of kindness
5. Exercising
6. Living life instead of buying things
7. Living in the moment - mindful meditation
8. Time with friends

Unleashing Human Potential

A lot of people ask me what I do professionally, and when I tell them that I'm a dentist, the typical reaction is, "Oh, you fix teeth."

If only it were that simple.

One of the big reasons I got into dentistry was because I realized the power that a confident smile can give someone. And I realized that when people have a smile they can be proud of, they show it a lot more.

I found that the more people smiled, the more confident they were and the easier it was for them to speak and communicate. These people had a higher self-image, and a better self-concept. And believe it or not, I found that the more people smiled, the more career and professional success they experienced and the more productive relationships they had.

So when people jump straight to "you pull teeth" once I tell them I'm a dentist—well, it's not nearly that simple. What I and everyone else in our office are in the business of doing is unleashing human potential. We help our patients regain their ability to smile, and by doing so, we also help them acquire confidence, capability, and allow them to be more ready to take on the opportunities in the world and achieve great success for themselves and for their families in the process.

Case Study: What Yearbook Smiles Tell Us

Over the course of thirty years, Drs. LeeAnne Harker and Dacher Keltner followed the lives of one hundred women after graduating from college to determine if a positive emotional expression in their yearbook photo was linked to their life outcomes.

During the study, Harker and Keltner, along with their research team, contacted the women in the study at ages twenty-one, twenty-seven, forty-three, and fifty-two, asking them various questions about marriage, family, and work, among other topics. What they found was that "over time, women who expressed more positive emotion in their yearbook pictures became more organized, mentally focused, and achievement oriented, and less susceptible to repeated and prolonged experiences of negative affect." In addition, they confirmed theories that "individual differences in positive emotional expression were linked to personal stability and development across adulthood, the impressions and reactions from other people, and the marital satisfaction and well-being up to thirty years later, "adding that, "People photograph each other with casual and remarkable frequency, usually unaware that each snapshot may capture as much about the future as it does the passing emotions of the moment."[11]

Overcoming Fear with Practice

Now that you understand the fear, the consequences, and the motivation of a healthy mouth, let me share with you how we're working to change the dental experience forever. The first and most important step is education—knowing the *why* behind regular visits to the dentist—but the next is on me and my team, which is to make those visits the absolute best they can possibly be. Doctors can't afford to continue with the old-fashioned model of making patients wait on them. Today, it's the complete opposite. Only those doctors that

---

11 LeeAnne Harker and Dacher Keltner, "Expressions of Positive Emotion in Women's College Yearbook Pictures and Their Relationship to Personality and Life Outcomes Across Adulthood," *Journal of Personality and Social Psychology* 80, no. 1 (January 2001): 112–124, https://doi.org/10.1037/0022-3514.80.1.112

are willing to put their patients front and center—to cater to *their* needs instead of the other way around—are the ones that are going to survive. And we intend to do more than survive—we intend to make your needs our number one priority, and in doing so, become *your* number one dentist.

Chapter Four

BEST TEAM IN TOWN

Over the years, I've spent a lot of time developing clinical skills, attending advanced training courses and doing everything I could think of to offer my patients the best and most up-to-date care possible. What I was missing, however, was the understanding that my team is the most impactful reflection of my ability. I could go through all the training in the world, but if lackadaisical staff members are treating my patients poorly, that knowledge and experience would never counterbalance that negative first impression.

Today, I understand that we have to stay at the highest possible level of clinical skills, training, and technology, not only to keep up with the rapidly evolving pace of dental technology, but to also provide our patients with the absolute highest quality of service.

The "best team in town" concept is our belief that we should not only have the most competent clinical team on the floor, but also a team that is present in all situations and circumstances, has been trained to stay focused on the patient, and a team that will never compromise on their work. This means that everything from the way appointments are scheduled when you call to how you're greeted when you walk in the door, how you're escorted to the treatment room, and even how you are communicated with should be top-notch and focused only on you.

It's Not a Job, It's a Career

One of our primary goals is to turn each role at our office into a career. This means reinforcing each team member's overall commitment to the practice and the patient, connecting them to the mission of our organization and encouraging them to apply our core values both personally and professionally.

Our Core Values

Our top priority is your quality of care.

We are driven to exceed expectations.

We pride ourselves on being on the innovative edge.

We are dedicated to our patients, community, and team.

Through modeling core values, it's our hope that our staff will have more of a positive impact simply through the behaviors they exhibit, particularly when interacting with patients and with each other.

In other areas, we strive to make a positive impact by providing our staff with the best training, coached in the understanding that we expect from them the highest level of commitment and expectation. As a patient, we want you to understand that we're taking all of these steps to dramatically improve your experience. Our training both in clinical skills and continuing education are not just a "bare minimum" effort, but are undertaken in order to stay ahead of the curve and at the top of our game.

One of these efforts ties directly into our desire to be a Patient-Centric office, which is engendering in our staff—and particularly our hygienists—the desire to not just treat patients, but to be their Oral Health Advocate.

Consider the following feedback we received from a hygienist shortly after going through patient-centric training:

The Honest Truth: *A Statement from a Veteran Hygienist*

The biggest problem that I see with other hygienists in other offices is that they aren't stepping up to the plate to be their patients' Oral Healthcare Advocate ... not just a hygienist. I'm not pointing fingers—I've been in those shoes.

I used to tell a patient what they needed to know about a procedure, and when they showed the slightest pushback, I would give up. I didn't know how to handle their irritation, their impatience, and their questions about financing, but I realized that was *my fault*. And because I didn't know how to communicate how big of an impact this decision was going to have on their life, they didn't get the care that they deserved.

As hygienists, if we don't step up for the patient, then we are the ones that are keeping a problem alive that has existed in the dental industry for way too long.

I still remember the day that this was made real to me. I was standing in the break room, drinking coffee and complaining about the training session that I and the other staff members had to take that day. We walked into the training room, all of us still highly skeptical. But then, the trainer started talking, and the truth of what she said hit me in the stomach. How she described the importance of advocating for our patients changed the way I looked at my career forever. From that day on, I knew I couldn't keep doing things the same way. I was no longer an "oral janitor" but an Oral Healthcare Advocate. My life's purpose is to give my patients healthier smiles and healthier lives, and to get as many other people to join me as possible. I'm telling you, I'm ready to start a revolution.

What I do is not just a nine-to-five job. It's not just a paycheck. Being a hygienist is our chance to serve—and to save lives. During my training, I realized that, as Oral Healthcare Advocates, we're literally the only people in our patient's lives that are aware of their oral health, so we can't be afraid to tell them what they need to do. Our patients trust us 100 percent to tell them what treatment is the best possible one for them.

As a hygienist, if you know that a procedure will benefit your patient, but you don't give 100 percent effort in educating them on it, then you are doing that patient a serious disservice. They don't know what you do, but they want to understand and they won't know what to ask unless you give them as much information as you can.

That's just the honest truth. If you're doing any less, then you aren't fulfilling your duties as a healthcare provider. It isn't that you have bad intentions if you don't—none of us do! Since becoming a hygienist, I've realized that the people in this industry are some of the warmest, most caring individuals I've ever met. But this epidemic of apathy has to stop. Some hygienists are out there doing the bare minimum of service rather than consistently over-delivering to their patients—being reactive instead of proactive about their treatment. I know that we can do better than that.

During training, our team learned to refocus on what each patient truly needs, and we made it our mission to give him or her the best solution. I now feel empowered to give my patients a healthier life and to take responsibility for that patient like I would a member of my own family.

Continuing Education

In addition to standard and continuing education, our staff may be participating in upward of one hundred hours of training per year on subjects directly related to the customer experience, such as the oral healthcare advocate training the hygienist spoke to earlier.

Our focus is on having a consistent process for everything from the front desk to the hygienists, to dental assistants, to the doctors in the practice. It's these processes that allow us to work with the other professionals in our office so that every patient receives the same, consistent quality of care.

Our Office is a "No Judgment" Zone

Let's address the elephant in the room right now—people judge. They judge us by our appearance, by the clothes we wear, by our opinions, even by the way we cut our hair. That may be able to slip under the radar at other establishments, but that attitude of judgment is left at the door at our office. If any one of our employees walks in with a judgmental chip on their shoulder, then that's the day they lose their job.

We do *not* judge anyone who comes to us. We do not allow any unchecked personal opinions from our team members drive how you are treated. We don't treat you differently based on what type of insurance you have or if you don't have insurance—we're simply interested in understanding what it is you need or want to have done, making sure you're comfortable, and providing you with what you need.

As a doctor, we want our patients to understand that this is not a normal commitment, but it is one that I believe is key to the relationship we share with our patients and the reason why our number one source for new patients today is referrals from existing ones.

Chapter Five

STEWARD OF YOUR SMILE

Let me ask you a question—have you ever worn down your tires and gotten a flat?

If so, what did you do? Did you go to the mechanic and ask for a patch, or did you get a new tire?

A lot of us have opted for the patch—even when the tires are so worn they're practically bald because we tell ourselves that we just can't afford new tires right then. When that happens, however, what do we end up doing? Eventually we have get that new tire, but we're spending more for it because we've had to pay for the patch and any other damage that happened to the car from running on bald tires until we bought new ones.

More often than not, we do more damage and end up costing ourselves more when we choose to "patch" instead of truly repair.

It's the very same situation with your smile. Your teeth bear much of the brunt of your lifestyle. If you enjoy acidic beverages such as coffee, wine or energy drinks, then that enamel is getting worn down every day. If your diet is high in sugar, then your teeth are constantly being bombarded by bacteria, and that's even if you're brushing the recommended two times a day (which a staggering one in five people *do not* do).

Taking care of your mouth is more than just brushing—there's a lot more that goes into it, and yet so few of us are on the preventive side of smile care. For instance, tell me—do your gums bleed when you brush? Do you ever notice a little bit of a gap between your gum and your tooth when you feel around your teeth with your tongue? Or is there buildup on a tooth or two that you just can't get off with brushing?

All of these conditions—gingivitis, receding gum line, and plaque buildup, respectively—are signs you need to see your dentist as soon as possible, and yet so many of us ignore these kinds of issues until they start to hurt. And by then, the conditions have likely progressed to point where more involved treatments may be necessary.

It's the strangest thing! We could go see the dentist every six months, get our teeth cleaned, floss regularly, and let the dentist take care of minor cavities as they occur, or we could do as more than a third of Americans do and just not go to the dentist until those preventive conditions become a severe problem.[12]

Acidic and sugary drinks and snacks aren't the only challenges that our teeth face on a regular basis. There's also the impact of stress on teeth—grinding (also called "bruxism") is associated with anxiety

---

12 Lecia Bushak, "Oral Health Isn't Much Of Americans' Concern, Poll Finds: One-Third Didn't See The Dentist Last Year," Medical Daily, last modified April 29, 2014, http://www.medicaldaily.com/oral-health-isnt-much-americans-concern-poll-finds-one-third-didnt-see-dentist-last-year-279468

and depression, and can cause you to wear away your enamel and expose the dentin, which is much softer than the enamel and can lead to sensitivity and cavities.[13] It could even cause your teeth to crack and, over the long-term, it can lead to complications with your jaw joint (also called the "TMJ" or temporomandibular joint) and may even cause facial muscles to become enlarged from overuse, potentially blocking your salivary glands, which then can lead to inflammation, pain, and dry mouth … which leads to more cavities, and so on.[14]

We define stewardship as "protecting and growing the owner's assets with fierce intensity." Therefore, taking stewardship of your smile is about recognizing that your health is a valuable belonging, and taking those preventive measures is paramount to maintaining your oral health so you never reach the point of paying $10,000 for a repair that could have been a minor fix if you'd seen your dentist on a regular basis.

When you do run into those repairs, though, stewardship is also about making the best choice for your smile rather than the cheapest one. Remember the tires analogy? Patching your problem ultimately ends up costing you more than getting it right the first time. And as your dentist, I never want to encourage you to just patch something five or six times when we can eliminate the problem once and for all.

13 Angelina R. Sutin et al., "Teeth grinding: Is Emotional Stability related to bruxism?" *Journal of Research in Personality 44*, no. 3 (June 2010): 402–405, https://doi.org/10.1016/j.jrp.2010.03.006

14 Donna Pleis, "Teeth Clenching And Grinding Can Affect Your Dental Health," Bruxism, Colgate, last modified, http://www.colgate.com/en/us/oc/oral-health/conditions/bruxism/article/teeth-clenching-and-grinding-can-affect-your-dental-health-1114

Why We Don't Care Who Your Insurance Carrier Is

When it comes to your health and your smile, my first thought is always going to be "What's the right thing to do here?" It's about what we can do to protect you and help you grow and live a full and happy life. If a close relative comes to me with a dental condition, for instance, I'm not going to tell her how to patch it for now—I'm going to tell her how to fix it for the long-term. And the same goes with my patients—I don't want to recommend temporary repair when you will be far better served in the long-term by fixing it right the first time.

This is why we don't care who your insurance carrier is. Ultimately, your insurance is never going to give you everything you need. We accept it, but if it costs more, then we'll find a way to make it work. Financing is readily available and there are ways to make it affordable. But insurance should never be the deciding factor. We are taking care of *you and your family*, not your checkbook, and how well you take care of your mouth impacts every aspect of your life from the day you're born and will follow you to the grave.

What Is the Cost of Neglecting Your Dental Health?

Health is an interesting value. It's something we all need and yet, it's not something we can purchase. We can't walk into a gym and say, "Okay, I'll take two well-defined biceps, a washboard stomach and a set of toned glutes. How much will that be?" Instead, we have to work hard to produce and maintain a healthy body on our own.

It takes time and it takes discipline, but for the sake of our overall health, it's worth it.

When we say "worth it," however, what do we mean? There's the personal, innate worth, of course—the cost of time and effort put into brushing our teeth or hitting the gym are "worth" it when it leaves us feeling healthier. But there are also physical financial benefits to good health, as well.

One economics researcher, Michael Grossman put it well when he described human behavior regarding health: "Individuals inherit an initial stock of health that … can be increased by investment," adding that "Individuals 'choose' their length of life" when investments are made through direct inputs into that stock, such as medical care, diet, exercise, and recreation.

If you really enjoy reading into the process of creating economic models, then you should certainly check out Grossman's paper "On the Concept of Health Capital and the Demand for Health." Otherwise, I'll just get right to one of his conclusions, which is that when we take stock of our life (or, in this case, look at it like investing in stock), we can predict that the more educated people are about the benefits of good health, including longevity, the more proactive they'll be about obtaining it.[15]

Consider the following study conducted by a group in Scotland, who set out to determine whether or not a country-wide nursery toothbrushing program was not only making a difference in the longer term dental health of children, but if it was also saving money on dental costs down the road. Specifically, the study looked at the cost savings from improvements in the dental health of five year olds

---

15   Michael Grossman, "On the Concept of Health Capital and the Demand for Health," *Journal of Political Economy* 80, no. 2 (April 1972): 223–255, https://doi.org/10.1086/259880

through the avoidance of needing extractions, fillings, or other treatments due to decay.

The first step was determining the complete costs for filling or extracting a decayed primary tooth, and then on average, how many of those dental treatments were conducted over a ten-year period.

They found that not only did the dental treatments for five year olds decrease over time once the toothbrushing program was initiated, but by the program's eighth year, the expected financial savings alone were two and a half times the cost of the program.[16]

How, then, can we be proactive about dental health? With two simple initial investments:

1. Brushing and flossing at least twice a day

2. Visiting your dentist at least twice a year

That's all the investment you need to make on a stock that can have incredibly rewarding returns.

Opportunity Costs of Dental Health

Essentially, an opportunity cost is the choice that you give up when you make a decision. That is, when given the choice between "gum" and "a mint" and you choose "a mint," the opportunity cost is the gum.

When you expand on that idea, "opportunity cost" not only stands for the loss of one choice in preference of another, it also represents the long-term consequences of your choice.

If we stick with the gum/mint choice, for instance, by choosing the mint, we could, say, miss out on the longer-term benefit of

---

16   Yulia Anopa et al., "Improving Child Oral Health: Cost Analysis of a National Nursery Toothbrushing Programme," *PLoS ONE* 10, no. 8 (August 2015), http://doi.org/10.1371/journal.pone.0136211

chewing gum. If the gum was sugarless and the mint was not, we'd be taking a hit on calorie intake by choosing the mint (as well as doing just that much more potential damage to the teeth thanks to that extended sugar exposure). Extrapolate that even further and maybe chewing gum could have kept us from thinking about eating a snack—but by taking the mint, we experienced a sugar spike and now we're eating a burrito at 2:30 p.m. instead of taking a walk, and by the end of the week, we've gained three pounds.

Opportunity Cost of Dental Health

OPTIONS: *brush and floss teeth everyday* **OR** *don't brush and floss teeth everyday*

CHOICE: *don't brush and floss teeth everyday*

WHY? *because I don't have time*

COST: *new implants to replace the rotten ones $3,000 to $6,000 per tooth*

Opportunity costs can be subjective, but they can also be quite objective and practical. In this case, consider the opportunity cost of deciding not to brush and floss every day.

The mouth is the perfect breeding ground for bacteria, and not just one type, either—there are close to four hundred different species of microorganisms, mostly bacteria, living on every filmy surface and in every hard-to-brush crevice.

According to dental researcher Sigmund Socransky, "In a clean mouth, one thousand to one hundred thousand bacteria live on each tooth surface. A person who doesn't have a terribly clean mouth can have 100 million to one billion bacteria growing on each tooth."[17]

While a good amount of those bacteria and microorganisms are beneficial, helping to fight off disease-carrying microorganisms that try to enter the body through the mouth, the oral cavity can also house harmful bacteria that, if not brushed away, can eventually irritate the gums, causing gingivitis, which evolves into periodontal disease. At this point, some of the most direct results of poor dental health may occur, including bad breath (otherwise known as halitosis) and tooth loss.

I discussed several of the following related conditions in an earlier chapter, but they're important enough to bring up again as the stewardship of your dental health can quite literally mean the difference between life and death. Those open, bleeding gums provide instant access to the bloodstream, where their presence has been linked to conditions such as:

- **Dementia**: researchers following more than five thousand people for eighteen years found that those "who reported not brushing their teeth daily had a 22 percent to 65 percent greater risk of dementia than those who brushed three times a day." Another, smaller study on Alzheimer's has noted that the brains of those with the disease exhibited more bacteria associated with gum disease than those without the mental illness.

- **Endocarditis**: bacterial infection of the lining of the heart and its valves, causing inflammation and infection

---

17   Jane E. Stevens, "Oral Ecology," MIT Technology Review, last modified January 1, 1997, https://www.technologyreview.com/s/400012/oral-ecology/

- ***Heart disease***: wherein harmful bacteria make their way directly to the heart

- ***Stroke***: bacteria-related inflammation of arterial walls and blood clotting can cause the arteries to narrow and lead to stroke

- ***Rheumatoid arthritis***: periodontal disease can increase the pain caused by this disease

- ***Lung disease***: both pneumonia and chronic obstructive pulmonary disorder (COPD) can be worsened by harmful bacteria making its way from the mouth to the lungs

- ***Brain abscess***: as noted earlier in the case of the twelve-year-old who died from a decayed tooth-related brain abscess, bacterial infections of the mouth can be life-threatening if left untreated. [18]

It only takes about three days of not brushing for detrimental conditions to form. Once you pass seventy-two hours, the volume of bacteria will have reached the point where they're producing enough acid to carve holes in tooth enamel, and plaque may have solidified to the point where it becomes difficult, if not impossible, to remove without professional intervention.[19]

What, then, is the opportunity cost of choosing not to brush and floss your teeth at least twice a day? It could be the cost of a filling, an implant, dentures, your overall health and even, your life.

---

18   Lauren F. Friedman, "13 Awful Things That Happen If You Don't Brush And Floss Your Teeth," Business Insider, last modified February 14, 2014, http://www.businessinsider.com/what-happens-if-you-dont-brush-and-floss-your-teeth-2014-2

19   Jane E. Stevens, "Oral Ecology," MIT Technology Review, last modified January 1, 1997, https://www.technologyreview.com/s/400012/oral-ecology/

Steward of your Smile

In our office, we adhere to the stewardship model, which is to protect you, to help you make good decisions and to help you grow as a person through the things that we can have an impact on.

When it comes to treatment, first and foremost, we believe in being good stewards of our patients, their time, their financial resources, and all of the transactions that occur in our business, which means helping our patients steward over their decisions in a meaningful and productive way. This is because we've found that many non-patient-centric offices will guide their treatment path based upon what they think the ability of the patient is to pay. This is simply *not* the philosophy that we use.

Instead, we treat you as a person and make recommendations to you as though you're a member of our family and allow you to ultimately make the decision that's right for you. We believe in providing you with the best recommendation for your condition, and the only way to do that is to leave the question of funding out of the picture.

As I pointed out earlier, there are times when budgets require people to patch something, be it a leak in a pipe, a hole in a weak roof, or a tire. But when we think about that decision over the long run, patching is pretty much a guaranteed way to have the problem return, and likely in a worse way than the first time around. This is why we like to give patients the option to fix things correctly the first time since it winds up being more cost effective and better for the patient overall.

Take the leaking pipe, for example. Patched, it may work a little while longer, but when it starts to leak again, that leak will likely go unchecked for a certain period of time and eventually cause more damage than it did when it was patched. The cost then ends up being the cost of fixing the problem correctly and repairing the damage done in the meantime. So which is the more cost-effective solution?

Convenient Financial Arrangements

When we consider the financial part of any visit to our office, we always approach it with these words in mind: flexible and without fear. We don't want to avoid discussing it—it's something we'll need to talk about anyway, so why not get it out there? But we don't want it to be awkward or to become a barrier to working with us. For these reasons, we offer multiple options for patient financing, including flexible payment plans.

In all cases, we like to provide our patients with options because there are times when we need to patch, but we always make sure to provide all of the information for the appropriate fix, as well, and discuss financial options if the budget is a problem. Above all, it's important to us that we educate our patients on the conditions resulting from either decision, including the consequences of patching versus fixing something correctly. Ultimately, the choice is in the patient's hands inside of our practice.

Chapter Six

BEGIN WITH THE END IN MIND

Did you know that between the ages of twenty and sixty-four, adults average about seven lost permanent teeth? And about 10 percent of Americans between the ages of fifty and sixty-four have *no* teeth left?[20] That's a lot of tooth loss, and if you're thinking right now that this average loss is probably greater on the older adult end than the younger adult, consider the following statistics from the American Dental Association's Health Policy Institute:

- Young adults are the most likely to report problems due to the condition of their teeth and mouth.

- 35 percent of young adults have difficulty biting and chewing

---

20 Lauren F. Friedman, "13 Awful Things That Happen If You Don't Brush And Floss Your Teeth," Business Insider, last modified February 14, 2014, http://www.businessinsider.com/what-happens-if-you-dont-brush-and-floss-your-teeth-2014-2

- 33 percent of young adults avoid smiling due to the condition of their mouth and teeth

What was also surprising about that report was that only 37 percent of the adults participating in the national survey reported that they'd visited the dentist in the last year, and only 77 percent planned to visit one in the coming year. This, despite the fact that just about all of them (95 percent) agreed that regular dental visits keep them healthy and a majority (82 percent) believed that a straight, bright smile will help you get ahead in life.[21]

Okay, enough statistics. What it comes down to is that dental health is incredibly important at every age, and at every stage in your life, you risk dental health issues. As we age, the risk rises, which is why it's our job to remind you that the decisions you make about your dental health today are going to stay with you for the rest of your life. If you neglect your teeth now, chances are that you'll need more work later down the road and if you neglect those bigger repairs, then you might end up being one of those ten-percenters without any teeth whatsoever.

Coming back to the importance of good stewardship, not only is it beneficial to see your dentist regularly, but it's also important to know the kinds of dental conditions that you can expect with age as your teeth wear, and as any work you've had done begins to break down and your gums begin to recede.

For instance, I've been shocked to have people come in that undoubtedly need a crown on a tooth, and yet they accuse me or my staff of making up the fact that they need it. But if you think

---

21   "Oral Health and Well-being in the United States: Data & Methods," American Dental Association's Health Policy Institute, 2015, http://www.ada.org/~/media/ADA/Science%20and%20Research/HPI/OralHealthWell-Being-StateFacts/Oral-Health-Well-Being-Methods.pdf?la=en

about how cavities are cared for—cleaning out the diseased area and bonding in a filling every five to twenty years, depending on conditions—then after two, three, or even four decay removals and filling replacements, inevitably there won't be much tooth left to fill and a crown will be necessary.

We don't want this or any procedure to be a surprise to you. Instead, it is our job to teach you about the natural progression of dental care and at what stages you may expect to take some extra preventive steps to keep your mouth healthy over the long term.

You can eliminate a lot of pain, discomfort, and frequent visits to the dentist by being proactive about your dental health. Our goal is to educate you so that you never feel that we're trying to "get" you to do something you don't want to do.

Check out the chart on page 63. There, you can jump to the most common dental conditions that are occurring at your age. I would suggest that you read it so you can have a good understanding behind any of the suggestions we make to you the next time you visit our offices. If you choose not to take preventive measures, that's your decision to make. However, know that if you choose to neglect your teeth for long periods of time, then you should budget to fix your teeth and take care of any related health conditions that may arise because of that neglect.

The best way to think about this is to begin with the end in mind. As you near the end of your life, what kind of teeth do you want to have? If you're like most people, then what you want is to have real teeth and a real smile. And you can have that - if you first understand that it is your responsibility to achieve it. As dentists, we're simply your partner and a provider of solutions to help you achieve your goals. It's on you to take the actions necessary to make those goals happen.

P a r t T w o

Your Mouth at Every Age

Dental Expectations at Every Age

Childhood

Ages 0-6

Teaching proper toothbrushing

Treating common dental emergencies

- Knocked out tooth
- Cracked tooth
- Tongue or lip bite
- Toothaches
- Objects stuck in teeth

Fluoride treatment

Ages 7-9

First orthodontic visit

Establishing proper eating habits—avoiding sugary drinks and foods

Applying dental sealant (painted on child's 1st & 2nd molars as they emerge)

Pre-Teens and Teenagers

Reinforcing proper eating habits

Greater likelihood of cavities

Hormonal impact on oral health

Ages 20-39

Increased risk for gingivitis

Risk of TMJ pain due to:

- Tooth movement or other dental conditions
- Injury
- Craniofacial muscle spasms
- Rheumatic disease
- Other factors that cause the temporomandibular joint to shift

Stress impacts on oral health

- Tooth grinding
- Cracked teeth

Maintaining orthodontic adjustments (such as wearing a retainer after braces)

Ages 40-59

Increased risk of periodontal disease

Maintaining annual comprehensive periodontal evaluation

Old cavities may have to be crowned, or the tooth removed/replaced

Increased risk of obstructive sleep apnea

Maintaining preventive dental care

Dental concerns may seem to come up completely out of the blue, but more often than not, they've been around for a while—we either just didn't notice them before or chose to ignore them until the irritation or pain become too much to bear. That's one of the biggest problems with dental issues—you could have a cavity and not even realize it until it becomes so deep that it hits the nerve. Or you may have gingivitis and ignore that tinge of blood when you're brushing or flossing until it becomes a full on case of periodontal disease.

This is what I sometimes call the "treadmill of dental life." Decisions regarding your dental health can come at you so quickly that you have to make decisions that you don't want to make—such as extraction or surgery—because of the condition you're in. However, if you're consciously taking preventive actions on the front end, then that treadmill slows down and you either don't have to make those decisions, or you have a lot more time to consider your options because you're aware of the condition long before it becomes a serious issue.

In this section of the book, we'll look at many of the dental concerns that can occur over a lifetime and what you can be doing now to prevent them. Or, if you haven't taken preventive measures for some time (such as brushing regularly and seeing your dentist at least once a year), this section should give you an idea of what conditions to expect at your current life stage.

> For more information, or if you'd like to book an appointment, please call us at (440) 937-8878 or visit our website www.NagyFamilyDental.com.

Chapter Seven

CHILDHOOD

Everyone has a childhood memory of what their first dental visit was like, which is why parents today are looking to make that experience better. They want their kids to look forward to seeing the dentist, which is why one of the first things we tell new parents is to bring their children in by the age of one.

That may seem a little young, but think of it this way: when babies are born, their mouths are sterile. Within hours, however, they're colonized with organisms that will stay with them for the rest of their life. These bacteria, protozoa, viruses, and yeasts are mostly harmless, but once they settle in, they start building a habitat that's more welcoming to other, less-harmless organisms. Once a baby cuts those first teeth, the bacteria that's most likely linked to tooth decay—*streptococcus mutans*—is also likely to make an appearance.[22]

One of our biggest concerns when a baby's teeth first start to come in is that of Baby Bottle Tooth Decay, also known as "bottle rot." This condition typically affects the upper front teeth and is caused by prolonged exposure to sugar-containing drinks—including milk (milk contains 12 grams of naturally occurring sugar per cup, otherwise known as lactose). Prolonged exposure can occur when a child is put to bed with a bottle, or if they use a bottle as a pacifier, and that sugar is the best way to activate the rapid growth of *streptococcus mutans*.

When sugar is present, *S. Mutans* feeds on it, releasing acids that can eventually eat away at tooth enamel, making room for plaque to take hold, which bacteria latch onto and from there, begin forming new holes. The more sugar that's added, the more this condition spreads until the mouth's natural cleanser—saliva—can no longer wash it away.

Even though a child will eventually lose his or her baby teeth, these first teeth play a very important role in life. They are needed for developing clear speech, chewing, and will also help the adult teeth come in correctly.

The charts on the following pages depict primary and permanent tooth development at different ages.

---

22   Jane E. Stevens, "Oral Ecology," MIT Technology Review, last modified January 1, 1997, https://www.technologyreview.com/s/400012/oral-ecology/

Toothbrushing and Dental Health Care for Ages 0–6

Infants

- For babies whose teeth have not emerged yet, use a clean, damp pad or washcloth to wipe your child's gums after each feeding.

- Only place formula, milk, or breast milk in bottles. Do not fill them with juice, sugar water, or soft drinks.

- Do not put an infant to sleep with a bottle. Bottles should be finished before nap time and bedtime.

- If an infant uses a pacifier, only give them a clean one—do not dip it in honey or other sugar-containing liquids.

1–3 years old

- When your child's teeth come in, use a child-size toothbrush and no more than a pinch (about the size of a grain of rice) of children's toothpaste to brush their teeth until three years of age.

- Encourage drinking from a cup

- Encourage healthy eating habits

3–7 years old

- Brush your child's teeth with a child's toothbrush and a pea-sized amount of children's toothpaste.

- If your child wishes to brush his or her own teeth, make sure to supervise the process to ensure that all of the teeth are brushed and all of the toothpaste is spit out instead of swallowed. Supervision should occur until the child is between the ages of six and seven.[23]

Dealing with Common Dental Emergencies

As many times as you've warned your child not to climb on top of the monkey bars, or open containers with his teeth, or ride his bike too fast (I could go on, but if you're a parent, you know what I mean), dental emergencies still occur. Here are a few ways to deal with them when they come up:

- **Knocked-out tooth**: try to put the tooth back in its socket without touching the root. If you can't, then either place the tooth in your child's cheek next to the gum, or if you're worried about the child swallowing the tooth, place it in a glass of milk. Then call your dentist immediately.

- **Cracked tooth**: rinse the mouth with warm water to clean it out and give the child a cold compress to place against the side of the mouth to keep any swelling down. Then call your dentist immediately.

- **Tongue or lip bite**: rinse the mouth with warm water and apply a cool or cold compress to the affected area.

- **Toothaches**: rinse the mouth with warm water and gently use dental floss to remove any food caught between teeth, as this can be exacerbating the pain. Call your dentist as soon as it is convenient.

- **Objects stuck in the teeth**: try to use floss to gently remove it, but if that does not work, call the dentist. Do not try to

---

23 "Baby Bottle Tooth Decay," Mouth Healthy, American Dental Association, http://www.mouthhealthy.org/en/az-topics/b/baby-bottle-tooth-decay

use a sharp, solid instrument to remove the object as it may cause further damage.

"Colorado Brown Stain" and the Introduction of Fluoride

You've probably heard me or other dentists talking about the importance of using toothpaste containing fluoride at every age, including those first toothbrushing years. There are a lot of reasons behind this, first and foremost that, while fluoride is added to tap water, very few people drink tap water anymore, opting instead for bottled water or filtered water (note, however, that "activated carbon" filters do not remove fluoride. Only processes such as reverse osmosis and deionization can remove the mineral).

Secondly, bottled water can be incredibly acidic. A study published in the Journal of Dental Hygiene found that, of the fourteen commercial bottled water brands tested, ten were acidic, with a pH of less than 7.

"Dental professionals continually educate patients on the dangers of consuming acidic food and drink due to their potential to contribute to dental erosion and tooth decay," the study noted. "However, water is not typically categorized as acidic." In investigating the pH values as reported on each of the bottled water manufacturers' websites, the researchers also found that the actual values were lower (more acidic) than those reported.

So why is fluoride added to water?

The discovery of fluoride and its dental benefits ironically began with the problems that fluoride was causing. In 1901, a young dentist named Frederick McKay arrived in Colorado Springs, Colorado, with the intention of opening a dental practice. What he found when he arrived was astonishing—the residents of the town had dark brown stains on their teeth, some so significant that "sometimes entire teeth were splotched the color of chocolate candy." Eventually, the condition became known as Colorado Brown Stain.

Apart from the coloration, however, the staining didn't seem to be causing any harm, and in fact, after years of research, McKay found that these mottled teeth were very resistant to cavity formation. Additionally, he found that city residents whose permanent teeth came in and calcified before the stains set in did not develop the stains later, so the staining had to occur while the teeth were developing.

It was later discovered that incredibly high levels of fluoride in the water were causing the brown stain—a condition that became known as "fluorosis." But lower levels of fluoride didn't stain and actually appeared to be beneficial. Later on, studies confirmed that fluoride ions easily absorb into the surface of teeth where demin-eralization has occurred, and bond with the enamel. The bonded fluoride then attracts other minerals, such as calcium, to the damaged area, thereby strengthen-ing the tooth overall.

The next question to answer, then, was how the benefits of fluoride could be used without triggering the ugly staining caused by fluorosis. Decades after the cause of fluorosis was discovered, Dr. H. Trendley Dean, head of the Dental Hygiene Unit at the National Health Institute, began to study exactly how much fluoride needed to be in water before fluorosis occurred, and whether or not physically and cosmetically safe levels of fluoride in water would help fight tooth decay.

In 1945, Dean worked out a deal with Grand Rapids, Michigan, to safely fluoridate the town's drinking water over a fifteen-year period. After eleven years, Dean was able to confirm that children born in Grand Rapids after the fluoride was introduced were 60 percent less likely to develop cavities.

Today, fluoridation projects benefit more than 200 million Americans and fluoride can be found in just about every toothpaste brand on the market.

Ages 7–9: First Orthodontic Visit

The best time for a child's first orthodontic visit is between the ages of seven and nine. This may seem like an odd time since most children still have quite a few of their baby teeth at this age, but this is actually the perfect age to have a preliminary screening done to ensure that there are no issues developing, such as crossbites, over-, or under-bites.

If there is an issue, this age is also the ideal time to start Phase One Treatment, which focuses less on the teeth and more on changing jaw growth. The younger a child is, the easier it is to guide the jaw into a stable, ideal bite. Imagine how much more growth a seven year old has ahead of him or her, rather than a twelve or thirteen-year-old—when potential issues are caught during this window of opportunity, orthodontists can get a jump on corrections and reduce the amount of time that child will need to spend in braces later on.

Ages 6–12: Dental Sealant

Dental sealants are thin coatings painted on a child's first and second molars (which emerge around the ages of six and twelve, respectively) that fill in the deep grooves of the tooth to prevent cavities. According to the Center for Disease Control (CDC), "once applied, sealants protect against 80 percent of cavities for two years and continue to protect against 50 percent of cavities for up to four years." This is particularly important as the permanent back teeth are where nine out of every ten cavities occur.

---

*Top Three Tooth-Rotting Beverages**

Sports Drinks

Sweetened Iced Tea Drinks

Energy Drinks

*People always say "Don't drink soda because of the sugar," but the truth of the matter is that a sugar-free energy drink is worse for your teeth than a classic cola because it's more acidic. It's that combination of sugar and acid that does the most damage, but acid is ultimately worse on your teeth than sugar.

Chapter Eight

PRE-TEENS AND TEENAGERS

The pre-teen years are when you really reinforce the importance of brushing teeth twice a day on their own. At this point, your child should have already had his or her first orthodontist visit and may or may not be undergoing treatment to prevent a bite condition. Of all the things you can do for your child's dental health at this age, having sealant applied is one of the most important, if only for the long-term impact that this simple process can have.

Eating for a Healthy Mouth

When it comes to maintaining overall mouth health, diet and nutrition are just as important as good brushing habits. Diet (the food we eat) and nutrition (the nutrients in the food) both impact the health of our mouth differently. Diet has a local effect, impacting the integrity of our teeth, saliva, and the mouth's pH balance, while nutrition has more of a systemic effect, impacting the integrity of the jaw bone, teeth, and supporting structure of the teeth. That is, changing your diet will more directly affect your mouth health while changes in nutrition will also have an impact, but it will happen over a longer period of time and affect the greater structure of the mouth.

Where we often run into trouble is the overconsumption of what's called "fermentable carbohydrates," which are those added and naturally occurring sugars in food. The difference between fermentable carbohydrates and other carbohydrates is that the fermentable kind breaks down in the mouth instead of later on in the digestive tract, sticking around to feed bacteria and launch the decay process.

Fermentable carbohydrates come in obvious and not-so-obvious forms. There are those foods that definitely contain sugar, such as candies, cakes, cookies, sodas, and chocolates. And then there are the less-obvious: bread, breakfast cereal, bananas, crackers, potato chips, pretzels and even dried fruit.

Additionally, the "stickier" these fermentable carbs are, the worse they are for your mouth, as they latch on to the nooks and crannies of the tooth and feed the bacteria that produces the acid that eats away at tooth enamel. "Sticky" doesn't just mean gooey and gummy in the way raisins and licorice are sticky—it can also mean "gets stuck easily" in the way potato chip crumbs can become wedged between your teeth and stick around long after you've finished eating them.

What are the best foods to eat for a wholesome diet, good nutrition, and an overall healthy mouth? The Dietary Guidelines created by the U.S. Department of Agriculture and the Department of Health and Human Services is a great place to start:

A healthy eating pattern **includes**:

- A variety of dark green, red, and orange vegetables
- Legumes (peas and beans)
- Grains, at least half of which are whole (brown rice, oatmeal, whole wheat bread)
- Fresh, whole fruits
- Low-fat or fat-free dairy, including milk, cheese, yogurt
- Protein foods, including seafood, poultry, eggs, lean meat, nuts, seeds, and soy products

A healthy eating pattern **limits** saturated fats, trans fats, added sugars and sodium, and includes consuming:

- Less than 10 percent of daily calories from added sugars
- Less than 10 percent of daily calories from saturated fats
- Less than 2,300 mg of sodium per day

If alcohol is consumed by adults of legal drinking age, it should be limited to one drink per day for women, and two drinks per day for men.

Every diet should begin with a strong base of grains as well as a daily intake of:

- 2 1/2 cups of vegetables
- 2 cups of fresh fruit
- 3 cups of calcium-containing milk, yogurt, and/or cheese

- Proteins (meats, beans, eggs, nuts)

And when it comes to snacking, try to choose non-sticky, non-fermentable carbohydrates. For example:

Best choice:
- Cheese
- Protein (meats, beans, eggs, nuts)
- Milk products (no sugar added)
- Water

Okay choice:
- Whole fruits such as apples and pears (these contain natural sugars, but have enough water in them that the sugar is diluted and saliva can more easily wash them out of the mouth)
- Vegetables (while vegetables contain carbs, they don't have enough to be dangerous)
- Unsweetened carbonated waters (these often contain a small amount of sodium)

Worst choice:
- Candy
- Cookies
- Crackers
- Bread
- Muffins
- Potato chips
- Pretzels
- Dried fruit
- Bananas

- French fries
- Cakes
- Soft drinks and other drinks containing sugar, including fruit juices

Ages 13–19: Treating Cavities

When lunch consists of a trip to the convenience store for a soda and a candy bar, cavities are eventually going to be an issue. A lot of teenage boys are full on into not taking care of themselves, and while girls tend to do a better job of taking care of themselves and their dental health, cavities can still become an issue—particularly if you have a family history of dental conditions.

Even though kids should already be seeing their dentist twice a year, this age range is when a bi-yearly checkup becomes incredibly important. Cavities need to be caught early and treated before they lead to further tooth decay.

When it comes to fillings, preference in the United States has more or less shifted away from silver amalgam and toward composite fillings, though there are a number of filling options available, and the procedure itself is pretty simple.

Types of Fillings

Depending on your preferences, the extent of tooth decay, and whether or not you have any allergies to certain materials such as metals, there are a number of options for filling materials, including:

- **Gold**: While expensive, gum tissues actually tolerate gold incredibly well and the fillings can last in excess of twenty years. However, apart from the cost, gold fillings also take longer as they often have to be made to order by a third-party lab before they can be cemented into place. This can require multiple visits before the procedure is complete.

- **Silver (amalgam)**: Also a material that's pretty resistant to wear, silver fillings also tolerate the heat and moisture of the mouth well, are relatively inexpensive, and last an average of fifteen years. However, since they're dark in color, they're more noticeable. One of the major disadvantages of amalgam fillings is they do not bond to the tooth. Even a small amalgam puts your tooth at higher risk of fracture. Compositionally, most silver fillings are composed of mercury, silver, tin, copper, and other trace metals.

- **Composite**: This is increasingly the most used filling type as the color is much closer to the natural color of the tooth. However, they tend not to last as long as metal fillings, with an average lifespan ten years depending on care. One of the primary advantages of composite over amalgam is that it reinforces the tooth. Composite bonds to the tooth, making the tooth less likely to fracture than when an amalgam is used. An typically, fractured teeth means a need for more extensive and costly treatment. "Composite" is short for "composite resins," which is usually a combination of specialized plastics and a filler such as silica.

- **Porcelain**: Like gold, porcelain inlays typically need to be custom created by a lab and then bonded to the tooth. These fillings can be matched to the exact color of the tooth and can last between fifteen and thirty years. By nature, porcelain is also resistant to staining. These fillings, however, can be cost-prohibitive, with prices similar to the cost of gold fillings.

Basic Filling Procedure

1. The process of cleaning and filling a cavity begins with local anesthesia, which is used to numb the area around the tooth so that you don't feel pain during the process.

2. Then we clean out the decay using a small drill and shape the space so the filling will fit in tightly. If we're doing a bonded filling, we'll also etch the tooth with an acid gel before placing the filling.

3. Finally, we'll place the filling and polish the tooth to ensure that the filling is smooth and comfortable.

Cavities By Age

How likely are you to need dental care as you age? Check out these statistics from the United States National Health and Nutrition Examination Survey (1999 - 2004) on the percentage of adults in each age range with either a cavity, or missing or filled permanent teeth:

Ages 20–34: 85.58 percent

Ages 35–49: 94.30 percent

Ages 50–64: 95.62 percent

How Puberty (Hormones) Can Affect Your Teeth

Along with all the other changes your body goes through during puberty, one of the more overlooked ones is the change that happens with your gums.

Between the ages of eleven and thirteen, when puberty is most likely to occur, gum tissue becomes more responsive to the accumulation of dental plaque and may bleed and become inflamed more frequently. When these symptoms become more prevalent, the condition is generally referred to as chronic marginal gingivitis, or puberty gingivitis, and it's generally believed to be caused by the increased hormone levels that occur with puberty*.

Both males and females are susceptible to the condition, and its onset is believed to be predictive of the formation of more significant periodontal diseases later in life.

This is just another reason why good dental health is incredibly important in the pre-teen and teenage years, as proper oral hygiene today can be the difference between healthy teeth and gums for a lifetime.

Of note, the hormonal changes that can occur with pregnancy and menopause have also been associated with an increased risk of gingivitis and periodontal disease.

Chapter Nine

AGES 20–39

The college years are another span of life where cavities are more likely to appear. The typical college diet doesn't help, with late-night study snacks coming into play more often and the general neglect of leafy green vegetables in one's diet. College is also when gum disease starts to pop up, starting out with the light bleeding of the gums during brushing, which is caused by gingivitis. If left untreated, those irritated, inflamed gums can quickly evolve into full on periodontal disease.

The good news is that gingivitis is pretty reversible during this age range. If you can get back into regular dental visits, regular cleanings, and brushing your teeth at least twice a day, the inflammation can go away without any permanent damage. If, however, the gingivitis goes for too long untreated, then not only will your teeth need to be cleaned, but your gums, as well, which is a much bigger deal. Think of it as similar to the condition that your car would be in if you didn't wash it for five or six years. You can't just drive that kind of buildup through the car wash and expect it all to come off—you have to get some serious detail work done.

What are the signs of gingivitis?

That little bit of blood in your toothpaste every time you spit? That's not supposed to be there. Gingivitis is the swelling and irritation of the gingiva, which is the part of your gum at the base of your teeth, and if it's not taken care of quickly it can lead to tooth loss, periodontitis, and other serious gum diseases.

Apart from a bit of blood when you brush, other signs and symptoms of gingivitis include:

- Puffy, swollen gums

- Dark red gums

- Tender gums

- Bad breath

- Receding gumline[24]

Gingivitis begins most often with poor dental health. When the biofilm on teeth isn't brushed away regularly, it can build up to form plaque, and that plaque is what causes irritation. Then, as the plaque builds, it turns into calculus—otherwise known as tartar—which is much more difficult to remove than plaque and is a breeding ground for bacteria. Only a professional dental cleaning can remove calculus. If that calculus isn't addressed, it will begin to irritate the gingiva, causing irritation, which then allows the gums to bleed more easily.

---

24 "Gingivitis," Mayo Clinic, https://www.mayoclinic.org/diseases-conditions/gingivitis/symptoms-causes/syc-20354453

This bleeding then opens the door to more bacteria getting directly into the gums and the bloodstream, leading to tooth loss, periodontitis and the risk of those diseases we mentioned earlier.

What increases the risk of gingivitis?

Poor brushing habits are the most common risk factor for gingivitis, but other conditions can contribute to the risk, including:

- Dry mouth

- Poor nutrition

- Dental restorations that don't fit well

- Crooked teeth that aren't cleaned well

- Conditions that cause a decrease in immunity such as HIV/AIDS, leukemia, or cancer treatment

- Smoking or chewing tobacco

- Old age

- Hormonal changes

- Genetics

- Viral and fungal infections

Headaches or TMJ Pain?

Of all of the hinging points in your body, the temporomandibular joint (TMJ, commonly called the "jaw joint") works harder than any other. Also, due to the combination of sliding motions and hinging, the TMJ is also the most complicated joint in the body. The jaw joint is where all of the major movements of your skull are centered and it is constantly moving, whether you're aware of it or not. On a conscious level, its active when we chew, speak, or yawn, and on a subconscious level its constantly making micro movements such as clenching, grinding, shifting, and repeatedly opening and closing.

Due to its connection to the trigeminal nerve—the largest of the twelve cranial nerves which run throughout the upper and lower jaws and into the teeth, eyes, and even the tongue—the smallest misalignment can have a significant impact on the rest of the system.

There are numerous conditions that may lead to TMJ pain, many of which become more prevalent as we age. These include:

- **Tooth movement or dental conditions** – tooth movement as we age, the wearing down of teeth, and tooth replacement, as well as dental procedures that change how our teeth interact, can affect the TMJ

- **Injury** – trauma to the jaw joint, head, or neck can have long-term effects that may not be felt until months or possibly years after the initial injury occurred

- **Craniofacial muscle spasms** – caused by injury or medications

- **Rheumatic disease** – this condition, which refers to a larger group of conditions that cause inflammation, pain, and stiffness of the joints, such as arthritis, can affect the TMJ as a secondary condition.

Common signs of TMJ issues:

- Facial aches and pains
- Frequent headaches
- Tooth wear

- Numerous dental problems (broken teeth, crowns or history of several root canals)
- Aches and pains around the ear
- Tender or painful jaw
- Discomfort or difficulty chewing
- Popping, clicking or grinding noise in jaw joints
- Difficulty opening and closing mouth due to locking of jaw joint

---

A significant sports injury in your teenage years or early twenties, or a car accident that seemed to only result in a case of whiplash, may evolve into issues with the TMJ later in life as the damaged jaw joint deteriorates under the tension of the unbalanced system.

What causes TMJ Pain?

Any time your bite changes, it affects your TMJ, and anytime your TMJ shifts, it can put mechanical stress on your teeth. Think of it like a finely tuned engine—if anything becomes misaligned, however slight, it will put stress on the system. As the stress increases over time, the misalignment becomes worse until the whole system becomes noticeably and painfully out of alignment.

Patterns of dental problems on the back teeth in particular can be a sign of undiagnosed TMJ issues. These problems can include root canals, missing back teeth, cracked teeth, broken porcelain fillings, etc, any of which can indicate that the system is under more stress than it should be. Additionally, teeth that are under additional stress from excessive bite force are also more likely to suffer periodontal problems.

One of the biggest problems with TMJ issues is how long they take to manifest. If headaches due to an injury that affected the TMJ don't appear until years after the incident, then it's not likely that the person suffering from them is going to make that connection.

Good dentists should be on the lookout for these types of conditions. If the alignment of the patient's jaw seems off, even if it's just slight, and we suspect a TMJ issue, then the first thing we'll do is test the diagnosis. This typically involves the patient being fitted with a type of mouth guard called an occlusal splint, which sets the jaw joint back into an ideal bite when worn.

An occlusal splint may look like a standard mouth guard, but it does more than just protect the teeth from grinding together at night. Instead, it is custom designed to hold the jaw in just the right position so that the teeth are aligned, relieving the muscle stress being placed on the TMJ by the misalignment.

After a few days of wearing the splint, the patient will come back in and we'll discuss the impacts, if any. If the patient is feeling forty or fifty percent better just from wearing it, then we know we're headed in the right direction. If they still feel the same and the headaches aren't getting any better, then we'll continue to fix the tooth issues that they originally came in to see us about and we'll likely refer that patient to another doctor. While TMJ issues are an often looked-over source of headaches and facial pain, other causes include ear infections, facial neuralgias (nerve-related facial pain), and sinus problems.

If the occlusal splint *is* making a difference, then the patient may wear it for anywhere from a couple of months to a couple of years until the jaw settles back into proper alignment.

Home Care for TMJ Issues

If you suspect that you have TMJ issues, there are some steps you can take at home to relieve the discomfort:

- Ice packs applied to the side of the face, particularly just in front of the ear where the TMJ is located
- Make conscious efforts to keep your face relaxed with lips together and teeth apart
- Eat softer foods
- Take small bites and chew with both sides of the mouth
- Don't rest your chin in your hand
- Don't bite hard objects, such as pencils, fingernails, cuticles, etc.
- Don't hold phones between the neck and shoulder
- Avoid excessive or extensive movements of the jaw, such as big yawns or chewing gum.
- Practice stress-relieving techniques
- Do gentle jaw stretches or jaw massages. One approach is to place your thumb or fingertip in the small "notch" located about one inch in front of your ears and on the underside of the cheekbone. Gently pressing inward and upward in this spot and rubbing in soft circular motions may provide some relief.

If the TMJ pain continues, there are other options for treatment, though each should only be considered after assessing all of the pros, cons, and risks with your doctor:

- **Pain medication:** Muscle relaxers, pain killers and other medications as prescribed may help with the temporary relief of TMJ pain.

- **Dental adjustments:** This involves making changes to the teeth to bring the bite back into balance.

- **Botox**: Since Botox works by blocking the nerve signals to the muscles, it may provide temporary relief to sore jaw muscles when used in small doses, although this method is not approved by the FDA for use with TMJ issues.

- **Surgery**: While surgery is an option, it should be avoided where possible as there are no long-term clinical trials showing the effectiveness of surgical procedures helping with TMJ disorders, and the treatment is often irreversible.

- **Implants**: Artificial implants to replace jaw joints are also an option, but should also be taken under the same strict considerations as surgery.

For more information on discussions around TMJ treatments, visit the National Institute of Dental and Craniofacial Research's page on TMJ disorders: https://www.nidcr.nih.gov/oralhealth/Topics/TMJ/ TMJDisorders.htm

Stressed Out? Your Teeth Are Probably Feeling the Pressure

"I sheared off my front tooth," actor Demi Moore explained to *Tonight Show* host Jimmy Fallon during a show back in June 2017.

"I'd love to say it was skateboarding or something really kind of cool, but I think it's something that's important to share because I think it's literally, probably after heart disease, one of the biggest killers in America, which is stress."[25]

While stress doesn't immediately cause your teeth to fracture, loosen, or fall out, it can cause this kind of damage over time, with stress increasingly becoming more prevalent in younger generations.[26] Under high stress, people may forget to brush or floss, and may not have the time or even think to visit the dentist. The same conditions can also lead to increased cortisol levels in the body, and while cortisol in the short term has an anti-inflammatory effect, extended or exaggerated stress response can lead to cortisol dysfunction, which can result in widespread inflammation and pain.

Stress in America—Harder on Young Adults

According to the American Psychological Association (APA), stress is becoming more of an issue for younger generations (Millennials born between 1984 and 2004, and Gen-Xers born between 1964 and 1984), who report feeling the most stress and the least relief compared to older generations. As of the APA's 2015 stress survey, adults in America:

- Report stress levels higher than what they believe is healthy (3.8 on a 10 point scale)

---

25 Bruce Lee, "Demi Moore Lost Two Teeth To Stress, Here's How It Can Happen," Forbes, last modified June 15, 2017, https://www.forbes.com/sites/brucelee/2017/06/15/demi-moore-lost-two-teeth-to-stress-heres-how-it-can-happen/

26 "2015 Stress in America," American Psychological Association, http://www.apa.org/news/press/releases/stress/2015/snapshot.aspx

- Rate their average stress level as 5.1 on a 10 point scale (up from 4.9 in 2014)
- Were more likely to report experiencing at least one symptom of stress (78 percent vs. 74 percent in 2014)
- Were more likely to report experiencing extreme stress (24 percent vs. 18 percent in 2014)
- Reported higher incidences of illness, with:
  - 67 percent receiving a diagnosis of at least one chronic illness
  - 16 percent diagnosed with depression (up from 12 percent)
  - 13 percent with anxiety disorders (up from 9 percent)
  - 32 percent with high blood pressure (up from 24 percent)
  - 58 percent with obesity
- Millennials and Gen-Xers were more likely to rate money as a stress source
- 45 percent of Millennials say their stress levels have increased in the past year
- 39 percent of Gen-Xers say their stress levels have increased in the past year
- Young adults are more likely than other generations to engage in stress coping/management activities, yet one in four young adults say they don't feel they're doing enough to manage their stress.

Stress can also lead to bruxism, which is the medical term for teeth grinding. If you apply enough force to your teeth, over a long enough period of time, you can do significant damage. On average, a human can bite down with two hundred pounds of force per square inch, which is actually pretty powerful, and when you apply that kind of force regularly on just about anything, it's going to cause some damage.

To understand how that kind of pressure affects the mouth, consider how this part of the body is composed. The tissues surrounding the teeth, for instance, are basically tight strands similar to guitar strings, holding everything together. But when you put excessive pressure on guitar strings, what happens? They pop, which is basically what is happening to the tissues around your teeth when you clench and grind. This is why the gums start to recede around teeth affected by bruxism, as the forces cause those tissues to break. If those forces continue, they go on to wear away the enamel, exposing the dentin and creating access points for bacteria to get directly into the blood stream.

Bruxism can occur consciously or subconsciously, while you're awake or asleep, and may not be a concern for months or even years after it first starts to occur.

Signs of bruxism include:

- Dull headaches (especially in the morning)
- Sore jaw muscles
- Pain radiating from the ear
- Teeth sensitivity
- Chipped, cracked teeth
- Loose teeth

- Damage on the inside of the cheek from chewing or biting

- Indentations in the tongue

While bruxism is common in younger children, the condition is usually temporary and more likely due to allergies, teething, or misaligned baby teeth as opposed to stress. Most children outgrow teeth grinding by their teens.

If bruxism continues, or if you suffer from it as an adult, then the long-term pressure and grinding of the teeth can lead to chipping, cracks, and loose teeth that may eventually fall out, as well as the wearing down of the enamel. In severe cases, the enamel can become so worn that the underlying layer of dentin is exposed. This not only causes sensitivity, but the dentin, which is nine times softer than enamel, is much more susceptible to decay.

In rare cases, long-term bruxing can lead to the enlargement of facial muscles, which can block the salivary glands, leading to swelling, pain, inflammation, and dry mouth. And dry mouth alone is a major trigger for cavity formation as the lack of saliva means that the mouth doesn't have its natural means of regular cleansing available to it.

While stress can certainly result in bruxism, teeth grinding can also be related to sleep issues or any of those childhood conditions listed earlier, such as a misaligned bite or allergies. In milder cases, bruxism may not necessarily need treatment. But if the problem persists to the point of discomfort, jaw pain, and damage to the teeth, then one or multiple forms of treatment may be recommended.

Treating Teeth Grinding (Bruxism)

Dental treatment

Although dental treatment may help to relieve the effect of bruxism, it won't necessarily treat the cause. Some options include:

- **Mouth guards and occlusal splints**: mouth guards can protect your teeth from grinding directly against each other while you sleep, and occlusal splints can be custom built to keep your teeth in an ideal bite position, as well as prevent direct contact of teeth during sleep.

- **Dental correction**: if the degree of bruxism has lead to teeth becoming so sensitive that you can no longer drink hot or cold liquids or chew properly, then the teeth may need to be reshaped and restored in order to repair the damage.

Behavior modification

If stress is a likely cause of bruxism, behavioral modification and stress management may help:

- **Stress management**: learning strategies that promote relaxation such as meditation, may help to reduce anxiety, which may have a positive impact on bruxism.

- **Behavior modification**: if you're aware of bruxism and how it's manifesting in your jaw habits, then you may be able to change that behavior by practicing proper jaw positioning, as demonstrated by your dentist.

- **Biofeedback**: through the use of electrical sensors, you can view information on how your body is reacting to subtle changes, which may help in reducing those actions that result in bruxing. For instance, learning how to consciously control your breathing and heart rate can be a helpful calming technique, and learning how to effectively relax the mouth and jaw muscles may reduce the effects of bruxism, or help to eliminate it altogether if its main source is stress and muscle tension.

- **Lifestyle modifications**: some at-home methods for reducing the factors that contribute to bruxism can include:

  □ Taking relaxing baths, listening to soothing music or exercising

  □ Avoiding stimulating substances such as alcohol or coffee in the evening

  □ Getting a good nights sleep

  □ Asking your sleep partner to let you know if they hear you making any grinding noises, or if your jaw is clicking at night, so you can inform your dentist or doctor

  □ Schedule regular dental exams to spot signs of bruxism early

By addressing teeth grinding earlier in life, you're more likely to avoid its longer-term impacts, and more likely to make it into your later years with most, if not all, of your natural teeth.

Retaining That Smile

While this book isn't meant to focus on orthodontics, a lot of what happens as part of your orthodontist visits directly affect your dentist visits, and vice versa. For instance, if you had braces as a teenager, it's likely that your dentist played an important part in keeping your teeth clean between orthodontist visits and reporting any concerns, breaks or other conditions to your orthodontist.

After the braces come off, that relationship between orthodontist, dentist and patient continues as the patient is monitored to ensure that the braces did what they were intended to do—and a big part of that has to do with whether or not the patient is good about wearing a retainer.

It's a tough ask for a teenager who just got out of braces to continue wearing another appliance, but the first year after braces is vital for ensuring that the teeth are secure in their new locations. This is why your orthodontist likely recommended that you wear your retainer up to twenty-two hours every day for the first three to six months, then every night at least for the following six months. Most kids are pretty good about that extra year—its the time afterward that presents the most challenge.

If you wore braces as a kid, you should still be wearing your retainer at least three nights a week and ideally every night for the rest of your life.

This is because, even with all of that time in braces, your teeth are going to shift. It may take a couple decades, but your teeth will gradually shift forward and inward with age—unless you have gingivitis or periodontal disease, in which case your teeth will shift much sooner than that.

If, by chance, you have been wearing your retainer regularly since your teenage years, then the other caveat of maintaining that healthy straight smile is getting your retainer replaced as needed; every two to ten years, depending on how rough you are on them. This isn't just because the retainer can wear out, however—it's also because of the inevitable tooth drift that occurs as you get older. Even with retention, teeth are going to shift slightly and the retainer will need to be adjusted in order to keep those teeth in proper alignment. And if you need a new set and you no longer live near your old orthodontist, don't worry—any orthodontist can have a new one made for you.

Over the course of a lifetime, you may go through several retainers, but wearing a retainer a few nights out of the week is a small price to pay for the long-term benefit of keeping your teeth straight and healthy.

Chapter Ten

AGES 40–59

For most of us, that feeling of invincibility that we've had our whole lives is likely starting to wear off in this stage—and our systems are starting to wind down a little along with it.

On the brighter side, this is the stage of life where a lot of us start taking better care of our bodies. Before this age, parents in particular were putting their children's health ahead of their own, making sure the kids went to the doctor and dentist regularly while neglecting their own health. Once the kids start to grow up, moms and dads start to reinvest in making themselves look and feel better, working on getting their looks as close to—or better than—they were in their pre-kid days. This likely means more working out and more time at the dentist, looking into what can not only be done health-wise but also cosmetically.

Unfortunately, this is also the age when people who were neglecting the signs and symptoms of gingivitis are now likely suffering from full-blown periodontal disease.

What is Periodontal Disease (Periodontitis)?

Periodontal disease occurs when gingivitis isn't treated, and the gums pull away from the teeth, forming spaces that then become infected. In fact, the word "periodontitis" means "inflammation around the tooth." As the infection grows, the toxins and the immune system begin to break down the bone and tissues holding the infected teeth in place, eventually leading to tooth loss.

The signs and symptoms of periodontal disease are the same as gingivitis—as are the risk factors. Treatment, too, follows the same path, beginning with a complete deep cleaning that involves scraping the tartar from above and below the gum line, and removing rough spots on the tooth root where germs gather. In some cases, a laser may be used to remove all of the offending buildup.

Antibiotic and antimicrobial medications may also be recommended after a deep cleaning, but if the damage is too extensive, surgery is most likely the next step.

Surgical Treatments for Periodontal Disease

There are two main types of surgical procedures for periodontal disease. Depending on the extent of the damage, your dentist may recommend:

Flap Surgery

This procedure involves lifting back the gums to remove extensive tartar deposits, followed by suturing the gums back into place so that everything fits tightly. Once healed, the gums should fit snug around the tooth and the teeth may appear longer as a result.

Bone & Tissue Grafts

Sometimes flap surgery isn't enough, however, particularly when the disease has eaten away at the gum tissue and even the bone underneath. Bone grafting involves placing a piece of natural or synthetic bone in the area of bone loss in order to stimulate growth. In some cases, guided tissue regeneration may also be used, which involves placing a piece of mesh between the gum and bone that blocks the gum tissue from growing where the bone should be, giving the bone and connective tissue time to grow. A graft of soft tissue may also be used for gum loss, with synthetic material or tissue from another part of the mouth being used to cover exposed tooth roots.

The success of either procedure is entirely dependent on the patient, his or her risk factors and how well mouth health is maintained at home going forward.[27]

Believe it or not, one out of every two Americans over the age of thirty have some stage of periodontitis, which the more advanced form of periodontal disease. And in adults over the age of sixty-five, the prevalence is a little over 70 percent of all Americans.[28]

---

27 "Periodontal (Gum) Disease: Causes, Symptoms, and Treatments," National Institute of Dental and Craniofacial Research, last modified September 2013, https://www.nidcr.nih.gov/OralHealth/Topics/GumDiseases/PeriodontalGumDisease.htm

28 "CDC: Half of American Adults Have Periodontal Disease," American Academy of Periodontology, https://www.perio.org/consumer/cdc-study.htm

Half of American Adults have Periodontal Disease

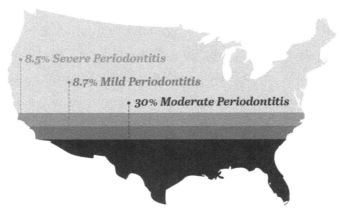

8.5% Severe Periodontitis

8.7% Mild Periodontitis

30% Moderate Periodontitis

47.2% of American Adults have Periodontitis,

that's **64.7 Million** Adults 30 years and older

Source: American Academy of Periodontology/Centers for Disease Control

Interestingly enough, according to a study conducted in part by the Centers for Disease Control (CDC), men are more likely than women to have periodontal disease (56.4 percent vs. 38.4 percent in women), and those at the highest risk include current smokers (64.2 percent), those with less than a high school education (66.9 percent) and those living below the federal poverty level (65.4 percent).

"Periodontal disease is associated with age," stated Paul Eke, MPH, PhD, lead author of the study and CDC epidemiologist, "and as Americans live longer and retain more of their natural teeth, periodontal disease may take on more prominence in the oral health of the U.S. Adult population. Maintaining good periodontal health is important to the overall health and well-being of our aging population."

With these findings, co-author Robert Genco, DDS, PhD, believes that periodontal disease should be elevated to the level of Public Health Concern. "We now know that periodontal disease is one of the most prevalent, non-communicable chronic diseases in our population, similar to cardiovascular disease and diabetes," Genco stated.[29]

Have You Had Your Annual Comprehensive Periodontal Evaluation?

According to the American Academy of Periodontology, every dental patient should have a comprehensive periodontal evaluation conducted on an annual basis to gauge periodontal health, diagnose existing disease, assess risk for disease, and determine any needed treatment. This service can be conducted during a regular dental visit by the general dentist, or by a dental hygienist or periodontist.

Crowning Moment

If you've had cavities since you were a kid, then crowns are very likely in your near future. Between the ages of forty and sixty is when most fillings have run their effective course. If you've been keeping up with your dental visits, then a cavity that you had filled in your pre-teens or teens was likely redone in your twenties or early thirties. Depending on the original size of the cavity, the redo of that filling will likely take away sig-

---

29 P.I. Eke et al., "Prevalence of Periodontitis in Adults in the United States: 2009 and 2010," *Journal of Dental Research* 91, no. 10 (August 2012), https://doi.org/10.1177/0022034512457373

nificantly more of the surrounding structure. Then, when the cavity needs to be replaced again in, say, ten to fifteen years, then there's a good chance that there won't be enough tooth structure left for a filling, and a crown will need to be placed instead.

The fact of the matter is that if you have a cavity, you're going to end up with a crown. It might be sooner, if the cavity is bigger or if you are particularly rough on your teeth, or it might be later—but it's almost always necessary.

Now is the best time for preventive dental care

It never hurts to remind yourself that your dental health down the road depends on how healthy you keep your teeth today. As you age, any problems you have today are going to get worse unless they're treated, and neglect today can result in new issues and problems tomorrow. Overall health can go downhill fast, and keeping your mouth young in old age requires diligence; brushing and flossing twice a day are more important than ever, and keeping regular dental appointments will ultimately cost you much less in the long run, as failing to see the dentist could mean bigger—and costlier—dental conditions down the road.

In addition, remember those conditions that have been linked in one way or another to overall mouth health—diabetes, heart disease, stroke and respiratory problems have all been tied to the risk of bacteria from gum infections slipping directly into the bloodstream and triggering inflammation in organs and tissues.

Want to make it into your golden years with as many of your own, real teeth as possible? Then today is the best day to start a proper dental care routine that will last you the rest of your life.

Chapter Eleven

AGES 60+

Cavities and lost teeth are a serious issue at this age, in part due to the long-term wear and tear on gums and teeth that has already taken place.

With an average bite of two hundred pounds of pressure per square inch, the human mouth is pretty powerful, but that power also has the ability to wear down on the outer layer of tooth enamel over time. And when you combine a lifetime of chewing and grinding along with exposure to damaging acidic foods and drinks, you run the risk of more cracks, breaks, cavities and overall damage due to that weakened enamel.[30]

Gum recession, too, is more common in older adults, with a little more than 70 percent of people over the age of fifty showing some

---

30   "The aging mouth – and how to keep it younger," Harvard Health Publishing, Harvard Medical School, last modified January 2010, https://www.health.harvard.edu/diseases-and-conditions/the-aging-mouth-and-how-to-keep-it-younger

degree of recession, and 90 percent with signs of recession over the age of eighty.[31] When this condition is left untreated, the exposed root is more susceptible to gum disease, which could eventually lead to the destruction of the gum tissue and even the bone around the teeth.

Although there's not much you can do to stop the natural wearing down of tooth enamel, keeping up with daily dental health habits such as brushing, flossing, and regular dental visits are as important as ever at this age.

Toothbrushing a Challenge? Go Electric!

Daily habits that we used to do without a thought can become more burdensome in our later years. Just brushing teeth, for instance, can be difficult if arthritis or other disabilities affecting motor skills are beginning to manifest. For those with limited dexterity, switching from a manual toothbrush to an electric one can make a big difference. Additionally, switching to fluoride toothpastes that aid in the remineralization of the teeth can help strengthen tooth enamel and fill in the weak areas that plaque tends to cling to.

Dry Mouth (xerostomia)

Because of the prevalence of medications being taken in this age range, for conditions ranging from diabetes to blood pressure to cancer treatment, dry mouth is a common occurrence. Not only does this usually result in bad breath, but the lack of the mouth's natural cleanser—saliva—means that cavities are starting to come back into

---

31   Claudia Hammond, "Is age the cause of receding gums?" BBC Future, last modified August 7, 2013, http://www.bbc.com/future/story/20130807-does-age-damage-your-gums

play, and habits to combat the condition, such as sucking on sugary cough drops or hard candies, aren't helping the situation.

Dry mouth can also be a problem for denture wearers, as the lack of saliva can make the dentures feel loose in the mouth, leading to discomfort. In these cases, a denture fixative and/or artificial saliva can help, as can drinking sips of water frequently throughout the day. Other options for combating dry mouth include:

- Chewing sugarless gum

- Sucking on sugarless candies

- Avoiding alcohol or caffeinated beverages

- Avoiding tobacco

Varnish for a Healthier Smile

Even though cavities may seem like something only kids have to worry about, the fact is that the rate of tooth decay for people ages sixty-five-plus is now exceeding the rate of cavities in schoolchildren.[32] Part of this is due to those two age-related conditions mentioned earlier: dry mouth and gum recession. As the lack of self-cleaning saliva becomes more prevalent and more of that soft root tissue becomes exposed, the risk of developing cavities increases, particularly along the gum line.

To get ahead of that risk, more dentists are beginning to recommend a fluoride varnish around the base, or neck, of the teeth. The varnish, which usually consists of anywhere between .1 percent and 5 percent sodium fluoride and a resin or synthetic base that helps it stick to the teeth, sets rapidly and can be applied quickly, reducing

---

32 "The aging mouth – and how to keep it younger," Harvard Health Publishing, Harvard Medical School, last modified January 2010, https://www.health.harvard.edu/diseases-and-conditions/the-aging-mouth-and-how-to-keep-it-younger

the time that the hygienist spends in the mouth and minimizing the risk of gagging or accidental swallowing of the product.

While the majority of studies into the effectiveness of fluoride varnishes in preventing cavities have been conducted on children, more researchers are beginning to look into its impact on older adults. For children, systematic reviews have proven how effective topical fluoride can be in preventing or slowing the progress of cavities. With older adults, recent reviews have also shown a reduction in root cavities, with fluoride varnish controlling root cavities better than brushing with a high fluoride toothpaste alone. The study concluded that fluoride varnishes on older adults, particularly those who have difficulty brushing, would benefit from varnish being applied to the base of the teeth three to four times a year.[33]

Dental Implants and Dentures

More and more, implants are becoming the norm over dentures when it comes to replacing missing teeth. There are multiple reasons why—the main one being that implants look and act like real teeth. This doesn't just mean being able to tear into a corn-on-the-cob anytime you want—it also applies to how the implant acts in the mouth.

With dentures, the offending teeth are removed from the mouth and nothing replaces them. Over time, the body resorbs the bone that the teeth were removed from since it's no longer supporting teeth, leading to the degradation and thinning of the jaw. Implants, however, are made with a material that bonds with the bone, acting like real teeth so that the body isn't stimulated to begin resorption.

---

33   Nicola Innes and Dafydd Evans, "Caries prevention for older people in residential care homes," *Evidence-Based Dentistry* 10, no. 3 (2009): 83–87, https://doi.org/10.1038/sj.ebd.6400672

Other benefits include comfort—implants act like real teeth instead of shifting in the mouth or requiring fixatives, as dentures do—and longevity. The typical implant has a failure rate of less than 5 percent and lasts an average of twenty-five years, with some said to last a lifetime. Meanwhile, the lifecycle of dentures is usually anywhere from seven to fifteen years.[34]

Implants are also a healthier option for the surrounding teeth, as well. When a bridge is placed, for instance, the two teeth adjacent to the area need to be ground down so they can hold the bridge structure. Consequently, these newly worn teeth are more vulnerable to decay and damage.

How are Implants Implanted?

The implant procedure typically involves placing a titanium screw in just the right place in the jawbone, followed by the attachment of the prosthetic tooth. In some cases, patients may opt for a combination of implant and denture, in which a series of titanium screws are implanted in the jaw, with the external end shaped so that a partial or full denture can be snapped onto it.

Implants don't work for all patients, however. If you smoke, have diabetes, or have substantial bone loss already, implants may not be the best option.

What to Know Before Whitening Older Teeth

As the outer layer of enamel thins, the dentin underneath becomes more visible, making teeth appear less white. Coffee, red wine, tea,

---

34 Lesley Alderman, "For Most, Implants Beat Dentures, but at a Price," Health, The New York Times, last modified July 30, 2010, http://www.nytimes. com/2010/07/31/health/31patient.html

and tobacco can also stain teeth, leading them to potentially look older than they are.

While over-the-counter whitening products and whitening toothpastes can help lighten teeth by a few shades, the effects are often much less dramatic in older teeth. However, before going through with a full-on dental whitening, keep in mind that professional whitening procedures may leave teeth feeling more sensitive and some stains may be more challenging to remove than others, requiring several rounds of bleaching before they can be removed.

Are Teeth Affected by Osteoporosis?

Osteoporosis, a medical condition that decreases the density of bones and makes them more likely to fracture, can also affect the bone density in the mouth. According to a study by the National Institute of Health, women with osteoporosis were three times more likely to have a loose tooth than women without the condition.[35]

Watching Out for Signs of Oral Cancer

As is the case with most cancers, the risk of oral cancer increases with age and the use of tobacco products. With each year that someone smokes or chews tobacco, the risk of developing oral cancer increases.

When oral cancer does develop, it's most likely to develop on the lower lip first, followed by the upper lip and then the tongue. Initial signs and symptoms of the disease are easy to miss, but if you notice a white or red patch on your lip, tongue, or bottom of your mouth that lasts longer than two weeks, let your dentist know about it. While

---

35 "Oral Health and Bone Disease," NIH Osteoporosis and Related Bone Diseases National Resource Center, https://www.bones.nih.gov/health-info/bone/bone-health/oral-health/oral-health-and-bone-disease

it may be the early signs of oral cancer, there's also the chance that it could be a sore caused by herpes or yeast infection, which, while painful, can also be treated.

Dental Care and Dementia

Older adults suffering from forms of dementia such as Alzheimer's disease should be allowed to conduct their own dental care for as long as they can, with reminders from family and caregivers, and supervision if needed. Establishing a daily care routine in the early stages of dementia is particularly important as assistance in brushing teeth may be needed later on.

Since it can often be challenging to communicate with someone who has dementia, it may be hard to tell if that person is suffering from mouth pain or discomfort. If you're a caregiver or family member of someone with dementia, it can help to keep an eye out for the following signs of potential dental problems:

- Refusing to eat hot or cold foods, or any food

- Frequent pulling at the face and mouth

- Increased moaning, shouting, or restlessness

- Refusal to take part in daily activities

- Aggressive behavior

- Disturbed sleep

- Not wearing dentures[36]

---

36 "Dental Care," Alzheimer's Society, https://www.alzheimers.org.uk/info/20029/ daily_living/9/dental_care/3

Dental Treatment for those Suffering from Dementia

According to the Alzheimer's Society, dental treatment for those suffering from dementia should be considered with all of the stages of dementia in mind. During the early stages, for instance, dentists should recommend and conduct treatment with the understanding that the patient will not be able to care for his or her own teeth at some point. Therefore, preventive treatments for conditions such as gum disease are very important. As the disease progresses, patients may need sedation or general anesthesia for dental visits, and their ability to co-operate during these visits should be assessed beforehand. In the late stages of dementia, the challenges of thinking clearly along with physical frailty and often additional complex medical conditions can make dental visits challenging, and care should mainly focus on maintaining the patient's comfort, preventing dental disease, and providing emergency treatment.[37]

When considering dental treatment for dementia patients, the following factors should be kept in mind:

- What dental problems are being experienced

- Whether the patient is able to give informed consent

- The patient's level of independence, thinking abilities, physical impairments, co-operation and mental state.

Once these conditions are assessed, the dentist can provide input on the best treatment options for the patient, and how regularly he or she should see the dentist.

---

37   Ibid.

As with every stage of life, keeping teeth in their best condition requires regular maintenance and common sense practices. With this in mind, a little effort now can make a big difference in the teeth you get to keep—and their overall health—down the road.

Part Three

Sleep Apnea and Snoring

Chapter Twelve

SLEEP-RELATED BREATHING DISORDERS

Do you snore? Does your partner snore, or your child? You may think of snoring as harmless, or even funny, but in fact, it's anything but. Snoring is the primary warning sign of a sleep-related breathing disorder. Obstructive sleep apnea (OSA) is the most common and the most severe sleep-related breathing disorder. A growing body of research shows that OSA can lead to all kinds of dangerous, even life-threatening, health outcomes. It is suspected that 30 to 50 percent of asymptomatic snorers will have some degree of sleep apnea.

How do I know if I've got Obstructive sleep apnea (OSA)?

Your sleep partner may be the first one to tell you. A person with OSA literally stops breathing for a few seconds when they're sleeping. Often, they'll gasp for breath, then go back to quieter breathing. These pauses in proper breathing are called apneas. This disruption may not entirely wake the person up, but it will move them from a deep sleep to a light, slight sleep, which greatly reduces the overall quality of their sleep. Other signs and symptoms that may signal OSA include

- excessive sleepiness,

- fatigue,

- memory impairment,

- mood disturbance,

- decreased libido,

- social withdrawal,

- cardiovascular disease, and

- nodding off at the wheel while driving.

People with sleep apnea may also gain weight, because the lack of sleep depresses their metabolic rate, and of course, additional weight can add to the apnea problem.

From the patient's point of view, though, the complaint I hear most often is how tired they are. It's no wonder, because effectively it's as though they spend the night running a marathon. Apnea cuts several years off your lifespan, and if it causes more serious health problems, you can lose a lot more than that.[38]

Sleep occupies a third of our life and good sleep is critically important to our health in ways you may not have thought about. The most important stage in sleep is stage three, which is known as deep sleep. This deep sleep is where a person's immune system and memory are both active. It gives your body the opportunity for physical and mental recovery, biochemical refreshment, memory consolidation, and emotional regulation.

Here are some of the critical functions that occur during deep sleep:

- Your blood pressure drops, leading to a more relaxed state.

- Your muscles receive more blood supply.

- Your body's energy is recharged.

- Your body starts to repair its tissues. At the cellular level, new tissue grows.

- The pituitary gland releases human growth hormone (HGH). HGH promotes cell repair and bone and muscle growth.

- Leptin, a natural appetite suppressant protein, is released

- Sugars and fats metabolize and help regulate body composition.

- Deep sleep consolidates our new memories and it also reduces the need for more rest.

---

38 "Obstructive Sleep Apnea and Obesity Hypoventilation Syndrome," John Hopkins Medicine, https://www.hopkinsmedicine.org/digestive_weight_loss_center/ conditions/obstructive_sleep_apnea.html.

- Adequate deep sleep may lessen insomnia and anxiety symptoms.

- Enough deep sleep gives mental energy and boosts cerebral acuity during the day.

- Your long-term memory is created during this time.

It is recommended that adults get between seven and a half and eight hours of sleep per night. Unfortunately, when someone has sleep apnea, they rarely get to deep sleep, and the effects can be devastating.

How common is sleep apnea? Estimates from the National Sleep Apnea Association suggest more than twenty-one million Americans compromise their health due to obstructive sleep apnea (OSA) with 80 percent of these undiagnosed. This is a health crisis and one we take very seriously.

What are the other predictors and conditions associated with OSA? They include

- cardiovascular disease,

- a lower jaw that is too small or is set too far back,

- the presence of hypertension,

- a Body Mass Index (BMI) of thirty or higher,

- a neck circumference of seventeen inches or larger for men and fifteen inches or larger for women,

- observed choking or gasping during sleep,

- inattention and changes in energy levels during the day, and

- enlarged tonsils and/or adenoids.

There is also evidence that some people who suffer from sleep bruxism—teeth grinding during sleep—may also have some degree of OSA, as that jaw movement may be related to the subconscious effort to keep the airway open during sleep, moving the jaw around or clenching it in order to activate the throat and neck muscles and keep the airway open.

Many people assume that if they're not obese and in otherwise good shape, they can't have apnea, but as the previous list shows, there are multiple issues at play in OSA. I recently treated a very fit and slender lady for it, so please don't dismiss the potential for apnea or any other sleep related breathing disorder based strictly on your appearance. Amazingly, there are even people who have apnea yet who don't report feeling the usual symptomatic tiredness that goes with it. But whether or not they feel it, they're still not getting the oxygen or the rest they need.

How is it diagnosed?

OSA is typically diagnosed using a polysomnogram (PSG) or a sleep study. During a sleep study, a sleep physician monitors brain activity and body system functioning while a patient rests overnight in a sleep lab. The specialist evaluates the study data collected to diagnose sleep disorders and recommend treatment. This diagnosis can also be done with a home sleep study.

While a PSG will measure dozens of factors while the patient is sleeping, one of the most important factors it will be measuring is the person's apnea-hypopnea index, or AHI. This measurement determines exactly how many apneas, or pauses in breathing, the patient experiences in an hour, as well as moments of shallow breathing called hypopneas. Additionally, the study will record oxygen saturation and count the number of respiratory effort-related arousals that patient experiences within an hour's time. These measurements, along with accounts of the patient's heart rate, airflow, air pressure in the esophagus, snoring, eye movement, and even carbon dioxide levels of the skin, are taken before presenting the patient with a diagnosis.

The Epworth Sleepiness Scale (ESS) (included on the next page) is a widely used standard screening form used to help diagnose a sleep disorder. Fill it out and tally your score. If it's higher than ten, that tells you that you may have a sleep disorder.

Apnea's impact on health

OSA can be rated as mild, moderate, or severe, depending on how many times an hour the patient stops breathing. Untreated OSA can lead to many serious health problems. Those with severe sleep apnea suffer heightened risk for coronary artery disease, congestive heart failure, and stroke, with apnea increasing the risk of heart failure by 140 percent, the risk of stroke by 60 percent, and the risk of coronary heart disease by 30 percent.[39] Untreated OSA multiplies the risk of developing Parkinson's disease[40] and increases the chances of developing cancer—according to some studies, up to five times the normal risk. Untreated OSA is linked to hypertension, coronary heart disease, atrial fibrillation, stroke,[41] type 2 diabetes, dementia,

---

39   Jean-Louis, Girardin et al. "Obstructive sleep apnea and cardiovascular disease: role of the metabolic syndrome and its components" *Journal of clinical sleep medicine : JCSM* : official publication of the American Academy of Sleep Medicine vol. 4,3 (2008): 261-72.

40   Yeh, Nai-Cheng et al. "Increased Risk of Parkinson's Disease in Patients With Obstructive Sleep Apnea: A Population-Based, Propensity Score-Matched, Longitudinal Follow-Up Study" *Medicine* vol. 95,2 (2016): e2293.

41   Jean-Louis, Girardin et al. "Obstructive sleep apnea and cardiovascular disease: role of the metabolic syndrome and its components" *Journal of clinical sleep medicine : JCSM* : official publication of the American Academy of Sleep Medicine vol. 4,3 (2008): 261-72.

Alzheimer's disease,[42] Gastroesophageal reflux disease (GERD), asthma, fibromyalgia, kidney problems, and weight gain. Studies indicate that someone with untreated severe OSA will die an average of seven years earlier than someone who does not have OSA.

In the recent years there have been concerns with complications of pregnancy and their relationship to OSA. Sleep deprivation in pregnant women significantly raises the incidence of pregnancy-related diabetes and doubles the risk of pre-eclampsia[43] and even increased incidence of infant and maternal mortality. It has been shown that pregnant women who have OSA deliver newborns with lower than average birth weight and lower Apgar scores.[44]

How is apnea treated?

There are several possible treatments for sleep apnea. The gold standard is what's commonly called the CPAP (Continuous Positive Air Pressure), which significantly reduces apnea hypopnea index (AHI). CPAP works by continually blowing pressurized air through the airway to keep the tongue and throat tissues from collapsing and blocking the airway. This air is delivered via a fitted mask. If the patient can use it, the CPAP is the best possible treatment.

Unfortunately, not all patients are able to tolerate the CPAP for a variety of reasons—in fact, many patients who are prescribed CPAP

---

42 Cross, Nathan E. et al. "Structural brain correlates of obstructive sleep apnea in older adults at risk for dementia" *European Respiratory Journal*, (2018): 52.

43 Patel, Soha and Judette M Louis. "Obstructive Sleep Apnoea in Pregnancy - More Questions than Answers" *European endocrinology* vol. 9, 2 (2013): 121-124.

44 Bin, Yu Sun et al. "Population-Based Study of Sleep Apnea in Pregnancy and Maternal and Infant Outcomes" *Journal of clinical sleep medicine : JCSM* : official publication of the American Academy of Sleep Medicine vol. 12, 6, (June 2016): 871-7, doi:10.5664/jcsm.5890.

machines simply stop using them.[45] Why? Mostly people complain that they're cumbersome, noisy, and not too comfortable. Some people report that the mask makes them feel claustrophobic, while others complain of oral or nasal dryness. Fortunately, there's another avenue for treatment in the use of custom-fit oral appliances.

What can your dentist do to help?

Thanks to our expertise in the structures of the mouth and jaw, your dentist may be the first person to spot some of the telltale signs of apnea and ask you about your sleep habits. Our training allows us to offer you education and treatment surrounding sleep health in the simplest and most cost-effective way possible.

The American Academy of Sleep Medicine recommends oral appliances as a primary therapy for the treatment of mild to moderate obstructive sleep apnea and for patients with severe sleep apnea who have been unable to use CPAP. The oral appliance works by holding the lower jaw forward so the tongue and throat tissues do not collapse and block the airway. And while not everyone can wear an oral appliance (children can't use them, nor can people with advanced periodontal disease) these are solving the apnea problem for many who otherwise would simply have had to live with it.

There are probably about fifty different versions of oral appliances on the market now, including some do-it-yourself versions that can actually do more harm

---

45   Norman Wolkove et al., "Long-term compliance with continuous positive airway pressure in patients with obstructive sleep apnea," *Can Respir J* 15, no. 7 (October 2008): 365–69, https://doi.org/10.1155/2008/534372.

than good. Of those on the market, there are about three that I think are good, but the best is one that was developed about twenty years ago by a Dr. Keith Thornton in Dallas, Texas, called the Thornton Adjustable Positioner, or the TAP appliance. Some years ago, I was fortunate enough to meet Dr. Thornton and spend several days with him. To this day we stay in contact with one another.

The reason I prefer the TAP appliance is that it's the most adjustable custom appliance out there, which means you're able to make very specific, small, and incremental corrections in moving the lower jaw forward. This ability to make minute alterations is important because we don't want to move the jaw any further than is necessary. And it's not a complicated adjustment; the TAP appliances adjust at just one point, whereas other appliances have to be adjusted bilaterally, with two different screws, which makes it trickier to get them right.

A well-adjusted TAP can help even severe sleep apnea, sometimes eliminating it altogether. For those who can't tolerate the CPAP, it can be a literal life saver.

That was the case with one of my patients, a young man with severe apnea who is confined to a wheelchair and can only sleep on his stomach. Because of that, he couldn't wear a CPAP mask. We made an oral appliance with him, and after some delicate adjustments and customization, it was a tremendous success. One of the great aspects of the TAP appliance is that you can make gradual adjustments over time, which helps to prevent other issues like jaw pain and/or TMJ.

Another patient of mine was an older gentleman. While his apnea rate was only slightly above normal, his wife of forty years couldn't stand his snoring and had relegated him to the guest room. He complained, too, of feeling tired all the time. At her urging he got a CPAP machine, but it just didn't work for him; he had terrible issues with nasal dryness and nosebleeds. He got an appliance from another doctor, but that wasn't a success either. When he came to me, I fitted him with a TAP appliance—and his problem (and his wife's) was solved!

Sometimes, jaw surgery is used to bring the lower jaw forward, widening the airway. Soft palate surgery, adenotonsillectomy, nasal obstruction surgery, weight loss, modifying your sleep position, myofunctional therapy, and pharmacotherapy are also possible options for treatment. Additionally there is a new procedure called Hypoglossal Nerve Stimulator that is described below by Dr. Kyle Schwab.

"A relatively new procedure has allowed for a high rate of success in OSA treatment. It involves implantation of a pacemaker. This pacemaker is much like one used for the heart but instead paces the tongue forward. The forward motion occurs only during sleep, as the device is activated when the patient is about to go to sleep. It is called a Hypoglossal Nerve Stimulator (HNS). It has shown great effectiveness for CPAP-intolerant patients, often lowering the AHI into a normal range. It is indicated for patients with an AHI between fifteen and sixty-

five. These patients also must have a body mass index that is less than thirty-two. This procedure is gaining more acceptance in the sleep medicine field as a good alternative for CPAP-intolerant patients."

—Kyle Schwab, MD, DABSM
Board-certified
Internal medicine/pediatrics/sleep medicine

Sleep Related Breathing Disorders in Children

Does your child snore or habitually breathe through his mouth? Science is just beginning to understand sleep apnea in children and its potentially devastating impact on their growth and development. If your child snores, you need to know that it might signal a serious sleep issue, just as it can in adults, and the health stakes are very high.

OSA is found in up to 10 percent of all children. Habitual snoring is seen in up to 12 percent of children.[46] Usually the tonsils and adenoids are the primary cause of airway obstruction. OSA in children can cause a multitude of health concerns. OSA in children has been linked to

- learning disabilities (ADHD and ADD) and other learning disabilities,

- bedwetting,

- inattentive behavior,

- hyperactivity,

- stunted growth,

---

46   James Chan, Jennifer C. Edman, and Peter J. Koltai, "Obstructive Sleep Apnea in Children," *Am Fam Physician* 69, no. 5 (March 2004): 1147–55, https://www.aafp.org/afp/2004/0301/p1147.html.

- accelerated weight gain, and

- anger or acting out.

The medical profession is only beginning to realize that many children currently being treated with powerful drugs like Ritalin or Adderall for ADHD may actually be suffering from apnea, the symptoms of which can present in exactly the same way.

Treatment for children can involve weight loss, adenotonsillectomy, craniofacial surgery, CPAP, and/or orthodontics. But the problem with the CPAP on a child is that the mask used puts pressure on the mid-face, which impacts the growth of the facial plates and all the bones. That can cause a mid-face deformity over time. And appliances like the TAP or others aren't really good for children either, because they're growing and their mouths are in flux, with teeth going and coming in. Fortunately, there's a new therapy available that uses a short-term appliance that doesn't create these kinds of issues. This is called the Healthy Start. It has just recently been introduced and is showing real promise.

We screen children for apnea via an examination of their mouth, and by using what's called the Ten-Item Sleep Screener (TISS) form (located on the next page). In the exam, we're looking for crowding at the back of the jaw, as well as at the appearance of the adenoids and tonsils. Sometimes, when the problem is a too-small jaw, it can be treated orthodontically with what's called a palatal expander that helps to expand the growing palate. It's all about the space: the less space you have in the mouth for air to flow through, the more likely it is that you'll suffer from apnea.

The Ten Item Sleep Screener

1. Does the child snore lightly or loudly at night?

2. Does the child exhibit excessive daytime sleepiness?

3. Does the child have difficulty falling asleep at night?

4. Does the child roll, kick, or move around frequently in sleep?

5. Does the child wake up frequently in the night?

6. Is the child difficult to awaken in the morning?

7. Does the child gasp, choke, or snort in sleep?

8. Does the child stop breathing during sleep?

9. Does the child get enough sleep at night compared to other peers of the same age?

10. Does the child have a difficult temperament (irritable or easily frustrated)?

If you've read this far, you have probably realized that sleep apnea isn't a condition you should just shrug off. If you suspect that you have apnea, please don't let your fear of either the diagnosis or the treatment keep you from seeing your doctor and getting properly screened. And if your spouse's or child's snoring, snorting, or gasping for breath is alarming you, get them in for an evaluation as soon as you can. Their life and health may literally depend on it.

If you've already been diagnosed, but your CPAP machine is in the closet because you can't tolerate it, you need to investigate the ever-improving options for treatment and talk to your dentist.

Recently, CPAP masks have been redesigned and improved in terms of comfort and should certainly be your first line of defense. But if you can't wear it, ask your dentist about other options for treatment. As I said, the technology is improving every day, and the chances are excellent that with one or a combination of treatments, your apnea can be successfully treated.

For more information, or if you'd like to book an appointment, please call us at (440) 937-8878, or visit our website www.NagyFamilyDental.com.

CPSIA information can be obtained
at www.ICGtesting.com
Printed in the USA
BVHW070914060123
655718BV00008B/710